D1132461

Perfect Phrases for Medical School Acceptance

Perfect Phrases for Medical School Acceptance

Hundreds of Ready-to-Use Phrases to Write Compelling Essays, Succeed at the Interview, and Stand Out from the Competition

Paul Bodine

New York Chicago San Francisco Lisbon London
Madrid Mexico City Milan New Delhi San Juan
Seoul Singapore Sydney Toronto

Copyright © 2009 by Paul S. Bodine. All rights reserved. Printed in the United States of America. Except as permitted under the United States Copyright Act of 1976, no part of this publication may be reproduced or distributed in any form or by any means, or stored in a database or retrieval system, without the prior written permission of the Publisher.

1 2 3 4 5 6 7 8 9 0   FGR/FGR   0 1 4 3 2 1 0 9 8

ISBN 978–0–07–159818–7
MHID   0–07–159818–9

This book is printed on acid-free paper.

McGraw-Hill books are available at special quantity discounts for use as premiums and sales promotions, or for use in corporate training programs. For more information, please write to the Director of Special Sales, McGraw-Hill Professional, Two Penn Plaza, New York, NY, 10121–2298. Or contact your local bookstore.

This publication is designed to provide accurate and authoritative information in regard to the subject matter covered. It is sold with the understanding that neither the author nor the publisher is engaged in rendering legal, accounting, or other professional services. If legal advice or other expert assistance is required, the services of a competent professional person should be sought.

—From a Declaration of Principles jointly adopted
By a Committee of the American Bar
Association and a Committee of Publishers.

Note: All the examples used in this book are fictional. The names of actual organizations and individuals have been used only for illustrative purposes and are not intended to accurately represent or characterize actual organizations or individuals.

Library of Congress Cataloging-in-Publication Data

Bodine, Paul, 1959-
  Perfect phrases for medical school acceptance: hundreds of ready-to-use phrases to write compelling essays, succeed at the interview, and stand out from the competition / Paul Bodine.
      p. cm.
   ISBN–13: 978–0–07–159818–7
   ISBN–10: 0–07–159818–9
1. Medical colleges—United States—Admission. 2. Essay—Authorship.
3. Exposition (Rhetoric) I. Title.
   R745.B63 2008
   610.71'173—dc22   2008036583

For Roberta and Claudia

Contents

Contents

Contents

Preface

Even in an age of dysfunctional managed care, inequitable health-care access, and ballooning costs, medicine remains one of the most respected and well-remunerated of professionals. Indeed, in 2006, almost 71,000 individuals took the Medical College Admission Test (MCAT), an all-time high, and in 2007, 42,315 applied to U.S. medical schools, the most in 10 years. Yet even with the addition of three more accredited medical schools in 2008, the number of available spots in medical school classes has remained relatively static. The most selective medical schools consequently know they'll receive enough applications with outstanding "numbers" (MCAT score and grades) to populate several entering classes. For this reason, they can afford to evaluate applicants in terms of the diversity and potential contribution they can offer potential classmates, not just in terms of their smarts.

This is where medical school essays come in. The personal statement required by the American Medical College Application Service (AMCAS) and the so-called secondary essays required by individual medical schools enable the admissions committees to look beyond your MCAT score, grade-point average, and résumé and see the person—to get a sense not only of what you have done but of the kind of person you are and the kind of physician you might become. Unfortunately, writing essays that showcase your uniqueness and potential contribution to best effect is not easy. Which of the many experiences of your life best capture your hopes, dreams, and strengths? What's the best way to tell these stories? The purpose of the "perfect phrases" in this book is to help you overcome the paralysis of the blank page (or PC screen) by giving you samples of effective medical school admissions writing that you can use to bridge the gap between your initial outline and your written draft.

Because generic writing is bad writing, you'll find that the phrases and examples provided here are not "one-size-fits-all" templates. They contain the concrete details—facts, names, places, numbers—that good writing always has. So feel free to use this book's perfect phrases as inspirational prompts, guides, even temporary "crutches" as you work toward a final draft that's expressed in your own words. But when you reach the point where you're confident in the substance of your essays—when writer's block is no longer an issue—search for ways to turn the perfect phrases you've used into your own personal expression. If you let this book's perfect phrases become a substitute for your own words, you'll defeat the purpose of this book and the admissions essay. Medical schools don't admit applicants who sound like other applicants or write what they think the schools want to hear. They admit real people who tell their own stories their own way. Use these perfect phrases to help you do that and only that.

Part I of this book guides you through the sometimes stressful process of writing admissions essays, from selecting your themes, developing your raw material, and preparing an initial outline, to writing, revising, and editing your drafts. The chapters in Part II provide perfect phrases for the most common medicine-related topics—from your shadowing and research experiences to why you want to go to medical school. The chapters in Part III cover the more general and personal topics—from the key challenges and influences in your life to what characteristics and experiences will contribute most to your medical school class. Part IV provides perfect phrases for the most common questions posed in medical school admissions interviews—a pivotal decision point in your journey to medical school.

It's my hope that the range and variety of examples in this book will help you to unlock and set free the inner creative voice that's still the best "magic bullet" for gaining admission to the medical school of your dreams. If you have any suggestions for improving it, please e-mail them to me at paulbodine@live.com.

Acknowledgments

Special thanks to Gigi Liu, Adam Lowry, Claudia N. Leiva, Erika Lebaron, Pawan Dhillon, and Daniel S. Thomas for their help. My thanks to Anya Kozorez of McGraw-Hill for bringing this book about and to my wife, Tamami, for her patience and support during this book's gestation.

Perfect Phrases for Medical School Acceptance

Part I

Getting Started

Chapter 1 Writing Medical School Essays

A s intimidating as writing medical school admissions essays can be, they offer you an irreplaceable advantage: they give you a crucial additional application component that you can fully control. From the themes you choose to encompass your personal "profile" and the stories you pick to illustrate them, to the lessons you draw and the tone you adopt, medical schools give you, through the personal statement and secondary essays, the reins to shape how they perceive your candidacy. Helping you structure and manage the potentially frustrating and time-consuming challenge of essay writing is the subject of this chapter.

Your Profile and Themes

Before you begin writing your admissions essays, you should first develop a short self-marketing message or "profile" that integrates the key themes (strengths, experiences, interests) you want your application to communicate. Take your time. Cast your net widely, and ask friends, family, and mentors for their input. You want to isolate the handful of themes or experiences—from your childhood, passions, or travels to your education, research, career, or community life—that will best distinguish you from other applicants. This profile is the guiding message that should inform all your medical school essays and indeed your entire application, from recommendation letters to the interview. When your application pools' test scores, grades, and demographics have all been sorted and batched, this is the "label" you want the medical schools to remember your application by.

Data Mining Your Life

Once you have nailed down your themes, you need to identify the individual stories that you'll build your AMCAS and secondary essays around. "Data mining" your experiences through conversations with family and friends, résumé-based brainstorming, or "stream-of-consciousness" writing (aka the "brain dump") can help you flush out these stories.

If you've done it right, your data-mining process should leave you with a mass of raw material that could fill dozens of personal statements. Now you need to evaluate your raw stories critically. Continually ask yourself which of the possible essay stories have the most value or significance. A story's external significance could include its impact on your life (such as an academic honor, research breakthrough, or job promotion) or on others' lives (such as showing compassion to a patient or helping to mentor children). A story's internal significance would include how the experience changed you, enhanced your skills, deepened your perspective, strengthened your sense of your potential, and so on.

Look for stories that capture in microcosm what's essential about you so you don't submit a "kitchen-sink" essay that superficially skims many key moments. By understanding these stories, someone can know as much about who you really are as by hearing your full autobiography. Look for the stories that are most distinctive and that combine the greatest external impact and personal transformation. If a story rates highly in unusualness, objective results or impact, and personal significance, you've probably got a winner. Subject all the raw stories generated by your data-mining process to this same weighing or ranking process until you've arrived at a core story or set of stories that you want your AMCAS and secondary essays to cover.

Essay Topics

The first and most important essay in your medical school application process is of course the AMCAS Personal Comments essay. As the Association of American Medical Colleges suggests in its application instructions, the likely focus of this 5,300–character essay are the following questions:

- Why have you selected the field of medicine?
- What motivates you to learn more about medicine?
- What do you want medical schools to know about you that hasn't been disclosed in another section of the application?

Notwithstanding the personal focus of that last question, medicine and its relationship to your future are the core topic of the AMCAS Personal Comments essay. For that reason, Part II of this book presents perfect phrases for the most common medicine-related topics, including shadowing experiences, clinical interactions with patients, research experiences, thinking insightfully about medical issues, and so on. Though the AAMC suggests that acceptable topics include personal information about you—"what hasn't been disclosed" elsewhere—it also restricts you to roughly 900 words. Many applicants will find that once they've finished writing about their academic and medical-related experiences, they have precious little space left to focus on "hardships, challenges, or obstacles"—or any of the other non-medical-related experiences that make them who they are.

Fortunately, in addition to the AMCAS Personal Comments essay, the secondary essays required by medical schools offer you a much wider range of topics and thus more opportunities to express the full breadth of your uniqueness. Glance at the essay topics in the applications packets of the 129 AAMC-approved medical schools, and you'll see several general topic areas emerge:

- Essays about personal material such as your upbringing, key experiences, and major life influences, including role models.
- Essays about challenges and/or disadvantages you've had to overcome (the same "hardships, challenges, or obstacles" referred to in the AMCAS instructions).
- Essays about personal characteristics or life experiences that might enhance a medical school's diversity.
- Essays about experiences that show your compassion or desire to help others.

We have devoted Part III of this book to perfect phrases for all these major personal essay topics.

Now that you have an idea of the topics you'll need to write about, we can get started on the essays themselves.

Writing Your Essays

The outline was invented to reduce the anxiety and time drain imposed by the writing process. By bringing structure to your personal statement before you start writing it, outlines maximize your efficiency and enable you to perform a crucial early test of the quality of your essay ideas. Do you have enough material to support your assertions or illustrate your experiences? Does the lesson or takeaway you're trying to draw from your story emerge organically from the story itself or does it seem imposed? Outlines can help you answer these questions before you've written a draft that you're emotionally invested in.

Let your creativity run as you write your medical school essays. At this stage, forget all the rules about transitions, "theme sentences" and "evidence sentences" that you learned in school. The real bottom line is this: essays will live or die by the degree of personal, vivid detail and insight you inject in them. Many applicants' essays never come alive on the page, and it's often because they lack specific human detail and personal anecdote. Always be as personal and concrete as you possibly can. You also want to achieve a balance between data—the facts that substantiate your themes—and analysis—regularly stepping back from an example or anecdote to tell the reader what it means.

First Drafts

Your focus when writing your essays' first drafts is really just to get something down on paper. Because many applicants believe they have to complete a polished, finished draft in the first sitting, they usually wind up with a starchy, formal-sounding treatise without life or detail. Don't be so hard on yourself. Again, forget about style, grammar, and word count when writing your first draft. Relax, run with your outline, and don't overanalyze what you're writing—just get it down.

It may help to think of your essays as stories about an interesting and sympathetic hero—you—who's in noble pursuit of a distant and holy grail (a medical degree). People are hardwired to respond to such human-interest stories. We like happy endings, and tales of sympathetic protagonists overcoming conflict or obstacles by changing their environments appeal to our basic hopes. Tell a good story.

Revising

Once you have written a rough draft based on your outline, step back and consider macro and organizational changes, such as contradictory themes or assertions, needlessly repeated points, gaps in context or logic, or weakly developed or poorly placed paragraphs. Continually ask yourself whether your main thesis and secondary points will be clear to the admissions readers, whether your words convey your personality and enthusiasm, whether you are telling your story as clearly, compellingly, and efficiently as you can. You may find that you need to switch around paragraphs, cut digressions, or add to, delete, or bolster your examples. Don't stress out. Remember, you already have your structure and rough draft; it's all downhill from here. Depending on how well conceived your outline was and how well you fleshed it out in your first draft, your essay may go through multiple macro-level revisions before it's ready for editing.

Editing

The next stage, editing, means cleaning up the essay's mechanics and grammar at the sentence and word level. The potential glitches that editing catches can be everything from pronoun and subject-verb agreement, dangling modifiers, run-on sentences, and faulty parallelism to punctuation and capitalization errors, word choice and misspelling, and active- versus passive-voice issues. One overriding rule that should guide your editing: always choose the simplest, shortest, and most direct expression over the more complex or "sophisticated" one. Read your essays aloud. Do they flow? Is the tone conversational? Does it sound like you?

Your essay is finished when you can't imagine how to make it say what you mean more candidly, vividly, or directly. When you've achieved that level of honesty, color, and tautness, let go.

Chapter 2 Perfect Phrases
for Introductions

L ike a smile and a firm handshake, a well-conceived introduction can create an instant positive impression in admissions readers that may pay valuable dividends when you later need them to sympathize with one of your failings or sit through a not-so-compelling example. Ideally your introduction will tell readers what you will be accomplishing in the essay, catch and hold their interest, establish your tone, and provide some of the context or detail that creates your story's foundation. Let your themes, specific story, and creativity suggest the introduction that works best for you.

The following perfect phrases will give you some idea of the variety of ways in which it's possible to open your essay:

- I first saw America from the inside of a hospital. Fifteen years ago my family and I escaped religious persecution in Vietnam to start a new life in the United States. During our three-week voyage to freedom, however, my brother Bao developed acute gastroenteritis from the rainwater we were forced to drink to survive. Without medical attention his life was in danger, so we spent our first two weeks in the Land of Freedom praying that Richmond Memorial's skilled doctors could pull him through. My first memory of America will always be the comfort and assurance that Doctors Weseltier and Gupta showed my brother and my family. They gave him his life again, which made our future in America possible.

■ "Failure to thrive." The phrase on Reed's chart seemed both coldly clinical and uncannily accurate. I first met Reed as a volunteer at Newark General Hospital when one of the nurses asked me to feed him his dinner while she tended to other tasks. When I peeked into Reed's room, I saw his two roommates eating their dinners with obvious gusto, but Reed seemed to be in a world of his own, oblivious to his surroundings and the meal before him.

■ "I got my ass whupped, but I am a warrior, and I will get those three guys. Just sew me up!" As soon as I heard Jim One Bull's words, I knew that the laceration over his left eye was less of a concern than the entrapped inferior rectus muscle he'd just referred to. Volunteering last summer at the U.S. Public Health Service's Indian Hospital in Clinton, Oklahoma, gave me a wonderful opportunity to witness doctors healing not only the damaged body, but the injured psyche.

- Washing the blood from Kimberlea's shoes was the least I could do. The 16-year-old had been waiting expectantly to be discharged at last from St. Louis Regional's ob-gyn emergency room when she suddenly began bleeding uncontrollably. Confused shock and horror swept over her face as she watched the torrent running. Dashing to her side, I escorted Kimberlea to a dilation and curettage procedure room, never letting go of her hand. As the physician performed a D&C on Kimberlea, I comforted her by gently stroking her hair. The procedure successfully concluded, I personally escorted Kimberlea to a bed and returned to the procedure room for her clothes. Seeing her blood-drenched shoes, I immediately began cleaning them—my routine tasks could wait. It became my guiding principle: do for patients what you would appreciate them doing for you.

- It felt like someone had jabbed a knife into my lower back. I was doing a routine "butterflies" exercise with 95 pounds of weight during college football training, when I felt my upper body suddenly freeze up and a wave of pain roll down my right leg. As I lay on my back wondering what had happened, I remember thinking that it was just a severe back spasm; I would be scrimmaging with my teammates in no time. I had no way of knowing that I had herniated a disk in my spine and would be living with debilitating pain for the next one and a half years.

- It's 7:00 a.m. in a rural hospital in Gansu province, China. As I clean a third-degree wound on a young girl, I hear a patient's gurney barreling noisily down the corridor. A fragile, panicked young woman is pushing her brother, who, thrown from his motorcycle, is drenched in blood and wincing at the pain from his broken nose and left leg. Though I'm startled to see that his blood has turned the entire pillow scarlet, I'm relieved that his coughs have forced the blood out of his nose, preventing coagulation in his lungs. But within seconds of his grasping my hand, his eyelids slowly shut, and he fades into unconsciousness. As his sister becomes hysterical, I summon the doctors, only to watch in shock and horror as they pass by the patient to ask me whether the sister has paid the $20 radiology and $100 hospital room fees.

- Wasn't leprosy an extinct disease like the Black Plague? Touring Thailand's Klongtuey Leprosy Center and Rehabilitation Hospital last November, my eyes gave me the answer. Though leprosy has been treatable for years, some one million cases still exist in developing parts of the world.

- The slimy, intricate viscera of a rat spilled out onto the operating table as Dr. Rubin Maslov proceeded to perform a tracheotomy. On my first day of research at Steerwright Laboratory, I silently marveled: How do the rat's parts combine to form the furry creature that was sniffing my hand a minute before it was anesthetized?

- "Go ahead—touch it." Stepping forward to peer into the patient's open heart, I was both awed and fascinated by the bright red muscle pulsing methodically under the glare of the operating room lights. It looked just like the pictures in the anatomy book I had read as a child. But this was real. Spurred by Dr. Wen's stories of open-heart surgery, I asked him if I could someday observe a surgery, and two weeks later I found myself scrubbing up with him and standing by as he opened the patient's chest. But Dr. Wen wanted me to experience the surgery more than just visually; he wanted me to physically touch the muscle. So, nervously, I leaned forward and extended a finger into the open chest. Suddenly, a stream of blood squirted from the pumping heart onto my surgical mask. The smell of blood permeated the OR, and I felt beads of sweat trickling down my forehead. The next thing I remember I was on the floor as a nurse waggled smelling salts under my nose. I couldn't believe I had just passed out! To my infinite gratitude Dr. Wen later assured me that mine had been a very common experience for first-time OR visitors.

- Two pounds, six ounces was the exact weight of little Anton when he was prematurely thrust into the world. As I stood outside the nursery window, I could see his tiny body barely visible beneath the tubes and electrodes taped to his pink-blue skin. Seeing Anton clinging frailly to life, I felt a swell of anger replace the fondness I had always felt for his 17-year-old mother. For six months, I had helped Jade prepare for the GED so she could support her new family. As her teacher, I was responsible for her academics, but I found myself more preoccupied with her health. Poor and uninsured, Jade did not seek prenatal care, and more than once I smelled alcohol and cigarettes on her breath. "No, I'm clean," she repeatedly vowed to me. Now, learning that Jade had been high when she went into labor, I felt betrayed because it was Anton who suffered from the actions his mother's lies concealed.

- "Do I live on the first or second floor?" Mrs. Moulton asked me one evening. I was astonished by her question. For the three months I had known her in my role as food server for St. Ignatius Home, Mrs. Moulton had always flashed me a bright smile that instantly nullified her advanced years and institutionalized surroundings. Through our always pleasant conversations I had learned that this distinguished but unassuming woman was a retired physician. Her question to me just now was doubly unnerving because it meant not only that she had forgotten where her room was, but that St. Ignatius has only one floor.

- You have a choice—your career or someone's life. That was the decision I seemed to be facing when I answered my phone at 2 a.m. on the day of my final presentation for my senior research seminar in Vanderbilt University's department of immunology and microbiology. But when the renal transplant coordinator at Davidson Memorial Medical Center, where I worked in kidney procurement and perfusion, called to ask me if I could assist in a kidney perfusion that morning, I knew I had to say yes.

- "Now what's he doing to Blake?" I whispered to my mom. For years Dr. John Stedelin, my pediatrician, was the last person in Centralia, Illinois, I wanted to see. As a child, I was blind to his compassion because I equated him with the throat cultures and painful immunizations I feared. But after my brother Blake was born, I would accompany him on his visits to Dr. Stedelin without being distracted by my dread of needles and swabs. My fear of Dr. Stedelin gradually evolved into a deep curiosity, something like the awe curious children feel as they watch a magician's illusion.

- "Brad, the camera crews are here!" my coworker called to me as the door opened behind her and news crews from the local TV stations filed into our laboratory. They had come to Syracuse University Medical Center to report a medical breakthrough: as part of the first comprehensive program in the United States to treat autoimmune diseases using bone marrow transplantation, our team had successfully treated a patient with systemic lupus using a new technique called *elutriation*.

- Virzenias was not very popular in our house. It wasn't his smoke-stained teeth, his macabre appearance, or even the vague scent of death on his clothes. It was the fact that his Sunday-morning phone calls meant my mother would not be with us for mass. As the autopsy technician who worked with my mother in her pathology practice at San Ysidro Hospital, Virzenias had the absolute power to call my mother away whenever an autopsy had to be performed.

- As I stepped into the dim "operating room," the first thing that hit me was the smell. As my eyes adjusted, I could make out Dr. Kutral removing the long iodoform wick from Sreela's left breast. In time I would learn to recognize that smell—pseudomonas infection. Sreela's eyes were pinched shut, but she made no sound. The size and shape of her nose ring told me she was of a low caste, and I knew she had been nursing her two-month-old boy from her uninfected breast because she was too poor to buy expensive formula. After repacking and dressing the wound, Dr. Kutral wrote Sreela a prescription, and she went back out to her crying son. Later, the doctor confided to me that Sreela would have to choose between the medication and food for her family. Reeling from what I had just witnessed, I walked out of the "clinic" (it lacked both running water and electricity) into the noisy, bustling village I would call home for the next five weeks.

■ "Code 10. Code 10." As I rush down to the cardiac floor to answer the call from a patient reporting chest pain, my own heart begins to pound as I review the procedures I will soon be executing with my first emergency cardiac patient: the initial exam, the subsequent tests and—if the situation worsens—the call for backup. I've just told the nurse to start the patient on oxygen and obtain a 12-lead EKG, and as I approach the patient's room I mentally review the possible scenarios. At best, the patient's chest pain is not cardiac-related; at worst, it is a manifestation of his already lengthy history of cardiac instability. This is the moment of truth—the first of many—medical school will prepare me to face and flawlessly handle.

- "Gross margin and P&Ls to gross anatomy and H&Ps." If I had to come up with a headline to describe the career shift I've made in the past year, that would probably be it. In the space of 12 months I've gone from analyzing the bottom lines of profit-and-loss statements as an equity analyst for T. Rowe Price to reading journal articles on "post-transectional axonal repair" as a post-baccalaureate premed student.

- The lines start forming at sunrise. By the time my shift as a volunteer at Ürümqi's Xinhua Hospital begins at eight sharp, a queue of cancer patients winds down Zunggar Street as far as the eye can see. After five summers of volunteering in New York City hospitals, when the time came for my January interim premed project, I knew I had to do something completely different. After several months' effort, my friend Kristen and I won permission from western China's two largest public health institutes to spend a month shadowing doctors and learning everything we could about China's public medical system.

- "Am I there yet?" I heard the resident ask from behind the curtain. "Do you still see bone on the drill?" the physician replied matter-of-factly. Horrified, I threw a quick glance at the patient's family, who—I thanked God—were too dazed with shock to understand what was unfolding on the other side.

Part II

**Perfect Phrases for
Medical Topics**

Chapter 3 Perfect Phrases for Shadowing Experiences

"Briefly describe the one healthcare experience that has had the most influence on your decision to study medicine."

(University of Miami)

"Briefly describe your exposure to medicine."
(Eastern Virginia Medical School)

How do you know you'll be a good doctor unless you've seen one in action? *Shadowing*—taking the time to follow a physician through her day to observe what her work is really like—may not be an official requirement for medical school admission, but it's certainly a de facto one. Seeing medicine come alive through the example of an experienced practitioner can tell you whether you'll enjoy a medical career, eliminate some of your false assumptions, and perhaps provide you with a mentor or role model you can turn to as your medical education and career begin in earnest. The following perfect phrases provide some variations on the shadowing theme.

■ At Dallas Memorial I have had the good fortune to interact with hematologist-oncologist Dr. Mark Gorecki, who early on allowed me to join him on weekend rounds at Irving Children's Hospital. I was immediately impressed with Dr. Gorecki's enthusiastic concern for his patients as well as the rigor and relevance of his research. Through him, I have been given the rare opportunity to interact with patients stricken with sickle cell disease, and I have been stunned by the amount of suffering and myriad complications these patients endure. I have also been humbled to learn that the discovery of the molecular mechanism of this terrible disease almost 60 years ago has provided little improvement in patient care. Most importantly, Dr. Gorecki has shown me that despite the social and economic differences that separate him from his patients, with compassion, enthusiasm, and warmth he can establish long-term trusting relationships with each of them. Through Dr. Gorecki, my attraction to medicine has evolved. While I was initially attracted to the problem-solving challenges it offers and because it would complete my understanding of biology, today I'm drawn to medicine because it gives me an outlet for compassion and caring, qualities inessential to research.

➥

■ After my volunteer experiences first sparked my interest in medicine as a career, I explored the profession further by shadowing a neurologist, internist, cardiologist, and radiologist in the Bay Area. I saw the hard work and sacrifice I had expected to see, but I also saw how much patience, compassion, and understanding—traits I had associated with the ministry—defined the healer's role. But it was only when I met Dr. Susan Cornelius, the Klongtuey Center's director, that I realized that choosing between the ministry and medicine was no choice at all—I could integrate both my Christianity and my desire to do more by becoming a doctor. A graduate of Scotland's most prestigious medical school, Dr. Cornelius had turned down lucrative jobs in the United Kingdom to come to rural Thailand and serve the leprosy center. She is now famous in Thailand as the brilliant doctor who runs a hospital for patients who can't afford even basic operations. Dr. Cornelius also began a policy of allowing one of the nurses to pray for patients before operations if they request it. (Christian or not, most patients do.) From Dr. Cornelius I learned that it was possible to practice a kind of medicine that treats the patients' emotional as well as physical needs. Under her I first realized that medicine is calling me and that I can handle its challenge.

- "In oncology you lose 50 percent of your patients." That is the hard truth Dr. Aaron Rom has been making sure I understand ever since I began shadowing him in 2007. Which half of those "even" odds would the smiling elderly man before me experience I wondered, as Dr. Rom and I entered the Atlanta Health Center exam room last summer. His body ravaged by arthritis and more recently lymphoma, Charles removed his too-large red cap with its "Jesus Saves" logo and smiled beatifically as his wife and son leaned forward to hear Dr. Rom announce the CT results: after two years of treatment, Charles was in remission. The emotion that suddenly filled that small room was unlike anything I'd experienced before. Since high school, I have been following Dr. Rom between exam rooms, hospital rooms, and intensive care units watching, usually awestruck, as he mixes honesty, competence, and concern for patient comfort to help dozens of families like Charles's beat the oncologic odds. Though I have mostly observed, Dr. Rom has taken the time to teach and explain, even allowing me to listen to lungs or feel tumors whenever possible. My time with Dr. Rom has been the source of my certainty that medicine is the only profession I want to pursue.
- Through my high school's health professions program, I was able to gain exposure to a different floor of

Union Veterans Hospital each week. That was how in late June 2007 I found myself shadowing a pulmonary technician named Atul Reddy. Responding to an ER call one day, Atul hurriedly invited me to join him. We sprinted into Room B–16 just in time to see a doctor thrust a tube down a frail-looking patient's throat. The lifeless woman had already turned pale blue; the monitor's constant buzz announced she had lost her heartbeat. My adrenaline surging, I watched anxiously as the doctor, Atul, and two nurses tried to revive her. After what seemed an impossibly long time, the monitor's high shrill turned into rhythmic beeps—the woman was alive! Exhilarated and relieved, I had to swallow my disbelief at the medical team's miraculous repudiation of death. With everything on the line, they had never hesitated, lost focus, or displayed nervousness at the magnitude of their task. I was awestruck, humbled, and, above all, inspired.

■ As they made the rounds in Larimer County General's geriatrics ward, the way the doctors I shadowed presented themselves to patients varied widely. One elderly woman suffering from dementia threw baleful stares and some choice obscenities at anyone who entered her room. Each physician seemed to have a different approach to gaining her trust, but some were more effective than others. Then Dr. Cydney Platt

➡

strode into the room wearing a glowing smile and radiating easy competence. Addressing the woman as if the two had known each other for years, Dr. Platt effectively disarmed the old woman with some salty humor and then listened to every comment she made with an expression of intent interest and concern. Clearly overwhelmed by Dr. Platt's charisma, the woman's combativeness melted away, and she became the model patient, docilely answering every question and acceding to every instruction. Dr. Platt was just as effective with other patients. On morbid patients who acted as if their slightest symptom was a harbinger of death, Dr. Platt would focus a blinding congeniality and air of supreme confidence that left each patient firmly optimistic about his or her condition.

■ I watched fascinated as the doctors we were assigned to examined patients' lymph nodes and administered bone marrow tests to determine which stage their cancers had reached. Although most had already progressed to later stages, the doctors did what they could, assigning the patients who could benefit from it to chemotherapy or radiation treatment. Most of the time, however, the doctors I saw were only able to answer their patients' pleading looks with kind words and a sigh of frustration that they had waited so long to seek treatment. Despite the obvious differences between the United States and China, when I think about my month in Karamay, I am struck by the basic similarity of Chinese and American doctors. The sacrifices in time they have to make to become practicing physicians, their commitment to their professions and to giving care, their ability to resist feeling discouraged, and the power of hope they instill in their patients—these cut through all the differences.

■ My career interest in medicine grew out of visits to my family physician, Dr. Thomas Maag. He was always happy to answer my questions about medicine, and with his encouragement I began volunteering at a Boulder-area hospital during my senior year. Knowing I needed to get a better idea of what a physician's career is really like, this past December I asked Dr. Maag if I could shadow him at work. He agreed, and for two weeks I accompanied him on 16-hour days as he treated patients and dealt with the challenges of a family doctor's life. Dr. Maag took time to give me the scoop on medical school, HMOs, and the financial side of the physician's career. More importantly, in everything he did, Dr. Maag showed me the deep satisfaction he gains from his work. He also helped me come to terms with the real side of medicine—human suffering. With his help I have discovered firsthand that death is a difficult but natural part of a physician's world. Yet when Dr. Maag introduced me to a patient whose entire lower jaw had been destroyed by cancer, I found that, though I could handle the patient's shocking appearance, it was deeply disturbing for me to put myself in the patient's emotional place. Sensing my struggle, Dr. Maag helped me see that the personal philosophy I developed for dealing with my sister's car accident was exactly the attitude that would help me deal empathetically with patients' suffering: "There are some situations you can't do anything about," he told me, "but you can always control how you react to them."

■ I was floored. During a health-care convention late last year, a Boston physician admitted to me that my psychology professor at the University of Houston, Anthony Medin, just might have helped more people day to day then most of the doctors in Houston. Doing clinical work with patients in Houston hospitals in addition to his teaching, Dr. Medin helped them cope with the psychological effects of their illnesses. Watching him, I learned that when patients master their minds, they can help heal their bodies. He showed me how an understanding of patient depression and the mental stages of illness can help physicians provide treatment that is specific for each patient. To truly understand and treat patients fully, we must also

➡

be able to understand not only their physical illness but also their mental perception of themselves. This is the lesson I will always remember Dr. Medin for.

■ "Clear the hall!" the nurse shouted as he rushed Xavier, lying pulseless on a stretcher, down the hall to the OR. On only my first day shadowing Dr. Sid Muroda, I watched as a dramatic effort to save a patient's life unfolded. As nurses and clinical technicians prepared the room for Xavier's emergency thoracic surgery, I heard someone shout, "He's been down for nearly three minutes." I looked over at Dr. Muroda, but he just waited calmly for Xavier to be brought to the table. As soon as Xavier was hooked up to the heart/lung machine, Dr. Muroda focused on his heart. As I stood transfixed nearby Dr. Muroda worked meticulously for the next seven hours, grafting coronary bypasses and replacing Xavier's malfunctioning left semilunar valve, which was riddled with calcium deposits. After he grafted the last vein, the moment of truth arrived. Would Xavier's heart beat on its own? For an interminable moment we all held our breaths for the answer. "Thu-thump." Miraculously, after seven hours, Xavier's heart began to beat independently again. When the surgery was over, the seriousness of Xavier's procedure was driven home to me when I accompanied Dr. Muroda to update Xavier's family.

➥

I could see the initial fear on their faces relax into relief as Dr. Muroda explained that Xavier had survived the surgery. But, he added, speaking gently but firmly, since Xavier was still in the coma that typically follows long surgeries, there was no way to know whether he had suffered brain damage. As his wife's eyes filled with tears, I learned my second lesson of that first day: being a physician not only requires the precise application of a vast amount of medical knowledge, but also the ability to compassionately handle the most painful interpersonal situations. Two days after Xavier's surgery he awoke from his coma with no apparent brain damage. When Dr. Muroda and I arrived in Xavier's room, he was sitting up wearing the kind of smile only a man who has cheated death can display. He shook Dr. Muroda's hand and simply said, "Thank you" while Xavier's family treated Dr. Muroda with a mixture of reverence and gratitude. I had spent only one day with Dr. Muroda, and I was already imagining myself as a physician.

■ I gained more clinical insights by shadowing Dr. Ralph Tehrani, a cardiologist, for three weeks in Nairobi, Kenya, in the winter of 2007. By observing him, I saw how doctors and patients interact, and I also witnessed the paradoxes of Kenya's health-care system. Dr. Tehrani's patients at Kenyatta National

Hospital were the country's more affluent, but he also volunteered at a primary care clinic in Kibera, providing services to Nairobi's destitute. Although he was a specialist by training, he was able to generalize his knowledge because it enabled him to serve a larger segment of people in Kenya's health-care system. My experience shadowing Dr. Tehrani crystallized my motivation to become a doctor. As a physician, I also intend to find ways to provide my services to all segments of society, including those who need it most but can afford it least.

■ What truly fascinated me about Dr. Goldberg were the memories of Dr. Hashemian that he revived in me through the compassion and caring he showed his tobacco-addicted patients. Through words of reassurance and patient answers to every kind of question, he tried to make them aware of the harm they were inflicting on themselves, yet without ever sounding judgmental. In other words, Dr. Goldberg was not only trying to heal his patients' physical ailments but, like Dr. Hashemian, trying to educate them with kindness. I began to envision myself as a physician like Dr. Goldberg—a doctor not only of the physical heart but the emotional one as well.

■ Whatever misgivings I had about medicine after my father's death were dispelled during my internship at the cardiology department of Austrian Saint George Hospital in Istanbul, Turkey, earlier this year.

As I followed Dr. Souroujon on his daily rounds, Mr. Demiray's bony body, covered with wires and tubes, always caught my eye. Mr. Demiray suffered from myocardial infarction and a failing respiratory system. He couldn't talk, but from the sound he made when he struggled to breathe and the look of defeat and hopelessness in his eyes, I could almost feel his pain. Several times, ready to give up, he resisted treatment, but Dr. Souroujon would speak to him patiently and encourage him to defeat the pain and trust in him. Dr. Souroujon never gave up. When Mr. Demiray left the intensive care unit two weeks later with his voice restored, he didn't say anything but, "sağ olun, doktora! [thank you, doctor]." Through his care and enthusiasm, Dr. Souroujon rejuvenated his patients, but he also revitalized my passion for the medical profession. He showed me that I can aspire to be a doctor who not only has a brain but a heart as well.

■ My interest in medicine has been profoundly affected by Dr. Patricia Capen. Before I met Dr. Capen, I was pursuing a medical career largely because I wanted to apply science in a "meaningful" way—though I wasn't quite sure I knew what that way was. Although I gleaned some insights into the profession from my father, it wasn't until I spent this past summer making rounds at the University of Minnesota Neurosurgery Clinic that I understood the real reason why Dr. Capen and my father had made such a commitment to medicine: they genuinely love what they do. I realized that I was no longer pursuing a career but a passion. And one reason why a physician's work doesn't seem like work is the gratitude patients show compassionate and competent doctors. I was inspired watching Dr. Capen, the brilliant and busy chairperson of the department, take the time to speak and listen to each patient as if there weren't another concern or person in the world. By showing patients this same attention and compassion, I can look forward to a medical career that's as enjoyable as it is fulfilling.

- "Take that to the lab, and let me know what kind of tree it came from!" Dr. Young joked as he handed me a leaf that he had just pulled from the helmet of the motorcyclist lying on the gurney before us. In an instant, the trauma surgeon's jest relaxed everyone in the room, including the patient. I then knew with clarity what being a good doctor is all about.

- My grandfather, Jarvis Kennedy, was a general practitioner who intuitively understood the connection between the psychological and physical realities of his patients' health. He practiced medicine in Deerfield,

Illinois, for over 50 years and got to know each of his patients, watching many of them grow up and bring in their own children for treatment. Last year, I listened with fascination as a neighbor of my grandparents told me of the time my grandfather treated a child with acute appendicitis. To save the child's life, Dr. Kennedy had to operate in his own house with minimal equipment. To help the child understand the necessity of this painful surgery, my grandfather talked to him at length until he was emotionally prepared for the surgery. It was Dr. Kennedy's ability to understand the child's anxieties and perceptions, and not only his physical and mental abilities as a doctor, that saved that young boy's life. For the past three Decembers I have also shadowed Dr. Elizabeth Scanlon in her orthopedic surgery practice in Seattle, watching her do everything from casting broken ankles to operating on fractured hips. Her efficiency and medical knowledge and the positive regard her patients have for her deeply impressed me. But I truly understood her devotion when she spent the good part of a Sunday afternoon exhaustively explaining and showing me how to cast up a broken leg. This summer I will be spending time with physicians in Cleveland and Detroit to learn even more.

Chapter 4 Perfect Phrases for Clinical Experiences

"Briefly describe your most important exposure to clinical medicine."

(University of Maryland)

"Please describe any experiences in a clinical setting (such as a hospital, physicians office, nursing home, hospice, etc.)."

(University of New Mexico)

While shadowing a physician is almost by definition a passive activity, clinical experiences show medical schools that you've also rolled up your sleeves and personally interacted with real patients in health-care environments—even if it was only to empty bedpans. Gaining clinical experience of some kind is even more critical than shadowing. You simply must do it. Fortunately, clinical experience can take many different forms, as the following perfect phrases suggest.

- When I was assigned to Barnes-Jewish Hospital's geriatrics ward a few months later, the head nurse told me to take the temperature and respiration rates of patients in Room 13. Introducing myself to my second patient, Eric, I told him what I was going to do. He nodded apathetically, but when I asked him how he felt, he began weeping. Baffled, I informed the nurse, and he said only, "He's been doing that lately." Disappointed at this response, I went back to comfort Eric and gradually learned the reason for his sadness. "I want to go home." Eric was simply lonely and homesick! I visited with him every day of his stay, and when he was discharged six days later, he turned to me and said, "Thank you very much and God bless you." I felt an indescribable surge of fulfillment and satisfaction. I learned that the best medication is often "simple" human warmth. Eric helped me see that I can really connect with people and help them feel better. That's when I knew that medicine was right for me after all.

- To interact more directly with patients, I began spending my breaks and weekends at the Pullman Township nursing home. As difficult and dirty as meeting residents' most basic needs can be, in doing so, I recognized the importance of such apparently trivial actions as brushing a woman's hair or making bedside conversation with a resident while cutting his Salisbury steak. I always laugh as I scoop up pureed pork or apricots for Mrs. Seaver because she closes her eyes and insists that I wait for her to guess which food I just put in her mouth. Even to residents who are unresponsive, I have learned to continue carrying on a cheerful if one-sided conversation. As I feed, dress, and clean the residents, I see the fading pictures on their walls of the people they were when they had spouses or young children. They are my reminders of each resident's humanity, and showing my personal touch and cheerfulness is my way of giving them the honor and care they deserve after 70 years of working, raising families, and giving to other people.

- I wanted a worst-case scenario to see if I was really up to the challenge of medicine. Dr. José Galvão told me of the Manaus Leprosy Hospital, and after much thought, I arranged to go there for six weeks last winter. Living out of a 7- by 7-foot room with no TV, phone, or Internet, I performed routine duties at the convalescent home such as cleaning, serving food, or just escorting blind patients during their walks. I had to tell the doctors that I could do more and hoped to learn more. To my surprise, they invited me into the surgical ward! I suddenly found myself prepping patients for surgery, which included washing the

➡

operating field with Betadine, helping the anesthesiologist, and applying tourniquets. During operations, which ranged from total hip and knee arthroplasties to amputations and spinal procedures, I helped the operating team by cutting suture threads or performing suction and retraction. Soon, I was also hammering orthopedic nails, inserting Orthopix screws, cutting with the saw, drilling holes, preparing bone fragments for bone grafts, and suturing and stapling—whatever the surgeon wanted. The work was not for the faint of heart. The instruments looked like relics from the Spanish Inquisition, and flying bone fragments, squirting blood, and the stench of cauterized skin were daily realities. I was accidentally stabbed with needles, cut with a saw, and punctured with a chisel. Strangely, not only was I not intimidated by this crash course in medical reality; I actually thrived on it!

■ "I named them Justin, JC, Lance—after 'N Sync." Antonne was talking about his T cells. Exhausted from his antiretroviral drug regimen, Antonne refused to discuss his future beyond one week. Every Friday for six months, I booked him in a residential hotel and transferred his grant money to his pharmacy, until one Friday, when he asked that I make his funeral arrangements. Antonne, like all 700 of Baltimore AIDS

Center's clients, had full-blown AIDS and was so disabled he could no longer work. Our not-for-profit ensured that grant funds supported clients during their unemployment. But once my clients' illnesses had progressed beyond early stages, how could I genuinely help them?

■ My role as a volunteer at Boca Raton Nursing Home was simple: I was to go around and ask the residents if they needed anything. To my frustration and disappointment, however, I discovered that after taking the time to get to know the home's Alzheimer's patients, when I came back 10 minutes later, I would have to begin the process of building trust and friendships all over again. Mrs. Erlbrunn was one of my favorites, a talkative woman who had shared with me her experiences living in a small Texas town where she was known as having "the bluest eyes anyone had ever seen." As much as I enjoyed her personality, listening to her forgetfully repeat her stories every time we met was a painful reminder of what Alzheimer's had done to this once vibrant woman. So I devised a strategy to inject a little excitement into her life. The next time I "introduced" myself to Mrs. Erlbrunn, I told her I had the mysterious ability to read palms. I held her wrinkled hand and started telling her about her small town, her high school days, and how,

➡

according to the secret knowledge I could divine from her palm, she was known for having the "bluest eyes anyone had ever seen." Mrs. Erlbrunn's delighted surprise—"How ever did you know that?"—was infectious, and in an instant three of her neighbors clamored, "Read mine too, read mine too!"

■ As a volunteer medical aide for a team of U.S. physicians organized by WorldCare Resources, I found myself surrounded by Ecuador's lush jungle, wild animals, and poverty unlike any I'd encountered before. The village's name, Las Casas, seemed cruelly ironic; its destitute inhabitants didn't live in houses but in frail shacks with cardboard mats for beds and barely enough food or utensils to cook a meal. I was shocked by the village's lack of schools, sanitation, and clean water and by the famished faces of the children who seemed to exist solely on Pepsis. But the most powerful image of my stay in Las Casas was the long line of villagers queuing up for medical attention at our makeshift clinic and the way my 26 WorldCare teammates and I responded to them. I had been warned that Ecuadorian medical care was minimal and that I would be working in a third-world environment, but nothing prepared me for the sight of a woman with an ovarian cyst so big she appeared pregnant, a man with a hernia so painful he ignored an enormous

➡

fungal infection around his ankle that threatened to leave him an amputee, or a young woman who could never lay on her back because a basketball-sized growth protruded from her spine. In my seven days in Las Casas I saw mental retardation, malaria, worms, tuberculosis, bony tumors, polio, and other physical disfigurements many Americans will see only in textbooks. Working 10-hour days, I filled medications at the pharmacy; screened long lines of villagers who had walked from miles away; explained patients' status to a surgeon, ophthalmologist, dentist, ob-gyn, and general practitioner; and struggled with my broken Spanish and pocket dictionary to explain prescriptions to patients and inquire about their complaints. My most unexpected task was to assist in the operating room. I scrubbed up and aided surgeons in a hernia repair, a vasectomy, and a gall bladder removal. But my toughest duty was to ask some patiently waiting villagers—some with four or five children all needing medical care—to come back the next morning.

■ During my stay in Romania I saw plenty of children with Burkitt's lymphoma and leukemia who were in desperate need of blood and food. To give the bedridden children a place to exercise and play, I built a playground area for them, which they received with warm gratitude. Only later did I learn that many of the children had been rendered paraplegic by the advanced stages of their illnesses. I saw many of these patients die, but the death of Mirela affected me the most. She was 14 years old and had leukemia. Despite her mother's heroic efforts to prolong her life, the doctors told us that she was not going to last much longer. We promised her a birthday party, with everything she ever dreamed about—a Barbie doll, a chocolate cake, a new dress. The party took place on a Saturday, and on Sunday they told us Mirela had died. Later her mother told me that Mirela had willed herself to hang on just long enough to enjoy the special moment of her birthday party before succumbing to her condition.

■ The summer before my junior year, I was offered an internship at the Center for Gynecology and Obstetrics in Varzob, Tajikistan. It was a "homecoming" I will never forget. I saw diseases and conditions that one very rarely encounters in the United States. The doctors had to deal with extremely limited medical supplies and medications, and gloves were resterilized to the point of disintegration. But for all the pride I felt in helping others in this impossible environment, it was not until I assisted in a delivery that I realized how right medicine is for me. I cannot describe the exhilaration and happiness I felt when I held that newborn baby girl in my arms, or how proud I was to sign my name on her birth certificate. During my three months in Varzob, I had the chance to assist in over twenty births, deliver five babies on my own, and assist in a number of other medical procedures.

■ "You will be a good doctor." Sometimes, if you hear something often enough, you start to believe it. As an emergency room volunteer at two Des Moines hospitals, I have camped with doctors and nurses in the trenches of medical care: restraining patients, calming people crazed with fear and uncertainty, and coping with extreme illness and death. Through it all, I learned that the healing power of the ER did not solely lie within the hospital's expensive tools and medications. Patients got the most comfort when they met someone who cared about them as a person and not as another medical case. This neglected aspect of medicine became evident as I transported patients to ICU, translated their Spanish to the English-speaking staff, and helped perform tests. One night an RN let me perform a pulse-ox test on a middle-aged patient named Marcus. I explained to Marcus that his results were normal and that he was going to be fine. We began to talk about personal interests, and gradually Marcus started to relax. As he was being transferred, he whispered to me, "You'll be a good doctor;

you'll be a good doctor." I was confused. I had simply performed a routine test on him; how could he say that I was going to be a good doctor? Later I realized that this man wanted to feel like someone was paying attention to him and not only to his illness. Being able to do that seemingly simple thing for him had earned me his trust.

■ I was a U.S. Army Special Forces captain on temporary duty in the mountains of Afghanistan during the last months of 2005. To help win the hearts and minds of the people who were "hosting" our stay, we planned to run a small aid station to give medical attention to anyone who wanted our help. As I walked down the dirt airstrip and entered the rear of our small compound, I had no idea what awaited me. At the aid station the turnout was overwhelming; the line of people—children, mothers, fathers, and elderly people—stretched for hundreds of meters. There were more people in line than lived in the small town! Obviously, word of this event had made it to other small towns in the area. No problem—all were welcome. An army doctor, a physician assistant, and a Special Forces medic provided the treatment, and with my limited medical training I helped out by taking brief histories, checking vital signs, and doing some translating. Most of the people were suffering from conditions like parasitic infections, malnutrition, upper-respiratory tract infections, and musculoskeletal pain—many conditions not seen frequently in the United States because of our preventive-medicine practices, diet, and personal hygiene. I learned more about medicine in two days than I had in any of my health science courses at West Point.

■ A few weeks later I found myself pushing open the rough-hewn door of a rural clinic in Gode, Ethiopia, 300 miles and several centuries from the nearest city. The work was life-altering. A queue of patients, suffering from malnutrition and other effects of poverty none of our four physicians could hope to cure, stretched for a block outside our makeshift clinic. For 10 hours a day, I helped a surgeon with ultrasounds, comforted female patients during checkups, and made evening house calls with doctors. I felt a woman's belly that was so full of tumors I knew she had little time left, though she at first did not. She left our clinic possessing the knowledge to make her own decisions about her final days. Though I'd left behind my car, my home, and all the familiar trappings of success, I never felt more complete. I left Ethiopia not knowing the words in Amarigna to express how tired I felt, but I was more certain than ever that medicine was my calling I was made for.

■ Every evening that I volunteer at Philadelphia's Advanced Practice Nurses Clinic (APNC) I walk into a waiting room filled with women and children exhausted and sometimes embittered by the hurdles their poverty has forced them to jump. Roshanda Washington is typical. Young, single, homeless, and slightly overweight, Roshanda is trying to find a job while raising her four children who are now playing in the shelter's after-school program. She has a history of hyperthyroidism and recently developed a goiter because the doctor visits and medicine are too expensive. She also suffers from depression. Listening empathetically, I introduce her to our mental health counselor and give her a referral to Thomas Jefferson University Hospital. As we talk about her life, I think about the surgery she will face if the medicine they give her doesn't work. At APNC I see the realities of a doctor's life, from scratches, coughs, and runny noses to congestive heart failure, HIV, and sexually transmitted disease. I perform simple medical procedures such as hemoglobin tests, blood sugar tests, and urine analyses, but I also provide preventive education about sex and drugs to teenagers. I sit with young girls as they wait, trembling with anxiety about the results of their pregnancy tests. I give emotional support to patients

➥

forced to live with worsening conditions because they lack insurance.

■ On my third day volunteering in the ER at the University of California San Francisco Medical Center, I watched as a multiple-gunshot victim was wheeled in and intubated. After one of the paramedics performed chest compressions, without a second thought I immediately took over the compressions while the paramedic gave his report. The physicians responded with rapid-fire instructions, and nurses quickly began administering medication. But the patient's chest cavity was filling with blood, and when a chest tube was inserted, blood gushed out of it onto the table, the floor, and those of us who were nearby. A bullet had shredded his aorta, and there was nothing more we could do. As the nurses began cleaning up, I noticed a piece of plastic on the floor. It was the victim's driver's license. That day he had just turned 21. As I stood there, the victim's license in my hands, my arms shaking with exhaustion, I learned my first powerful lesson about medicine: it will not always prevail.

■ During my month volunteering at the University of Pittsburgh Medical Center's Children's Hospital, I saw the pivotal role that pediatric physicians play both in educating, advising, and promoting healthy living during children's developmental years and in teaching their parents the habits that promote lifelong health. I still remember one young mother who tried valiantly to soothe her baby who was writhing and kicking in obvious discomfort in her arms. After the infant was examined and tested by our pediatrics team, I assured his skeptical mother that the disfiguring scaling plaques on her son's body would disappear once his zinc stores were replenished. After a day's supplementation, I was gratified to see the boy smile for the first time since his admission. Just as gratifying was the pleased look his mother gave me as she realized that my assurances of the day before had been confirmed. Of course, not all of our patients were fortunate enough to have such short stays or such happy results. But this early clinical experience showed me how good it can feel not merely to provide medical solutions but to see the raw gratitude of patients' families when you share the good news.

■ After graduating from high school in Russia, I enrolled in the seven-year MD program at Moscow State University. In my two years there, I not only learned a great deal about the medical sciences, but I also gained many valuable insights into the life of a medical student. Through the program—which offered an experimental problem-based learning curriculum—I learned basic science principles by solving clinical problems in the university hospital. In April 2006, I decided to broaden my education by volunteering for a patient support group as a commissioned Stephen minister—a layperson who assists pastors by helping care receivers through hospitalization, terminal illness, and other crises. The course I needed to earn my commission instructed me in how to care for the spiritual as well as physical needs of the care receivers and how ethnic background, religion, personality, and family affect patient recovery. While doing my rounds one day, I had the deeply moving experience of holding a "blue baby" suffering from tetralogy of Fallot. Hours of research helped me to gain an understanding of her heart condition, and after her surgery I was infinitely relieved to find that her heart defects had been repaired and that the cyanosis had disappeared. Her parents were both in the room and beamed huge, life-affirming smiles at me as if I had performed the surgery myself!

Chapter 5 Perfect Phrases for Research Experiences

"Describe your research experiences and indicate any interest in continuing with research in medical school."
(University of Alabama)

Since doctors need a basic knowledge of lab and research techniques, it's a good idea to describe your research experiences in applications to medical schools, especially those that are research-based institutions—and most of the top-ranked programs are. (If you are applying to an MD/Ph.D. program, you'll have to discuss research experiences because starting with the 2009 application year, the AAMC requires a separate 10,000-character essay on "significant research experiences" for dual-degree applicants.) Though medical schools favor hard science–related research, other research experience, such as public health or social science–related research, can also help. As the following perfect phrases show, you need to be able to discuss the focus or thrust of your research, your methods or approach, and the broader ramifications of your work.

■ Working as a medical technologist after graduation, I had the opportunity to participate in a bone-marrow transplant program at Massachusetts General Hospital in Boston. As a treatment option for cancer patients, bone-marrow transplantation enables patients to regenerate functional blood progenitor cells by engrafting healthy bone marrow cells. However, complete engraftment often fails because of graft-versus-host disease (GVHD). A relatively new technique, elutriation, prevents GVHD by reducing T-cells in the bone marrow graft through counterflow centrifugation, thus improving the success rate of bone-marrow transplants. After attending the elutriation training workshop at Johns Hopkins University Medical Center, where this technique originated, I was chosen in June 2005 to help implement this procedure at Mass General. Led by the oncologist of the transplant team, my team investigated various applications of the elutriation method, experimented with different approachest o setting up the operation system, and improved the original methodology by making successful modifications. We have since started clinical phase I trials to use this procedure to treat systemic lupus and multiple sclerosis, and most of our cases have been successful. Whether I was purchasing needed equipment with our limited budget or designing a closed system to avoid contamination, I was able to tackle each problem by constantly staying open to multiple angles of approach. My participation in Mass General's elutriation clinical phase I trials gave me the intense pride of knowing I was contributing to a better method for processing bone marrow.

- As the summer began, I was finishing my honors thesis on nutrition research for Professor Brenda Yu. Far from lab work alone, the project involved not only researching methods and nutrition policies but working directly with communities to examine their food systems and the challenges they face in commercializing food, using pesticides, coping with hunger, providing nutrition education, and supporting farmers' markets, among other issues. My role has been to examine the different stakeholders in community nutrition to see if people with a variety of backgrounds can reach consensus on a plan of action. I also evaluated the so-called Q-methodology—a type of survey technique that is thought to provide the same information as an extensive interview—to see if it actually correlates with qualitative research. Although work remains to be done, the project has taught me a great deal about the problems of food supply and hunger in rural and farming areas. Long-term solutions will require fundamental changes like boosting local economies, but so far the project has already convinced me that we can make a difference in improving communities' nutrition.

■ To deepen my scientific knowledge and apply some of the theories I was learning in class, I sought a "behind-the-scenes" glimpse at the ways research applies scientific methods to conquer disease. As a member of a research team in the microbiology and molecular genetics department at Carnegie Mellon, I have expressed the cloned forms of diphtheria toxin's A subunit in E. coli, and I am conducting experiments to assess their intrinsic nuclease activity. In the past two years, I have developed protocols for new research projects, evaluated team members' skills and progress, and presented my experimental results to my team members. I have learned that patience, perseverance, and an inquisitive mind are essential to scientific discovery. The more time and hard work I invest in research, the closer I come to understanding the mechanism by which the A subunit of the toxin binds and cleaves cellular DNA. Each successful project adds a small piece to the puzzle that will ultimately enable medicine to construct highly toxic "magic bullets" to target cancerous cells. I plan to continue this research as a lab technician in 2009 and compile my results in published form.

- Three summers ago I helped my UCLA thesis advisor, Dr. Mort Erdmann, conduct research into the development of ovarian cancer, which enabled me to first see the differences between research practices in Taiwan and the United States. As a biomedical research scholar at Taipei Microbial Genetics Laboratory during the summer of 2007, I studied the Heme biosynthetic pathway and the vertical transmission of human herpes virus 8, which is strongly associated with Kaposi's sarcoma. Then last summer, I spent three months in Borneo directly applying my basic research in a clinically relevant context. For about seven weeks, my days were divided between the lab and the maternity ward of the local hospital. Every day 30 deliveries had to be performed by only 3 doctors and 10 midwives, who coped without running water, trained support staff, adequate facilities, or medication. As I tended to the mothers and their newborns, I saw the suffering caused by years of guerilla war and poverty give way to happiness and gratitude.

- Volunteering at Cleveland Clinic's Cancer Center satisfied my scientific curiosity to investigate medicine at its most basic level. Applying the concepts I learned as a neurobiology major, I researched the role of telomerase in transforming normal glial cells into malignant gliomas, a brain tumor that even after surgical intervention offers its victims a life expectancy of only nine to twelve months. Is there a correlation between the malignancy of a glioma and telomerase activity? That was my research's driving question. After what seemed like an eternity of pipetting, I eventually found that over 95 percent of malignant gliomas I tested exhibited telomerase activity—a promising sign given that we may one day be able to target this enzyme for treatment. With the help of my advisor, Dr. Jacob Beauvoir, I then wrote an honor's thesis that enabled me to truly grasp the theoretical import of my research.

- At Duke University I got my first taste of biomedical research and wrote a thesis on the exciting area of tissue regeneration. In particular, my work attempted to isolate the genes responsible for regenerating auditory hair cells in the chick and to further understand why humans lack this regenerative ability. While I was finishing my master's degree, I was offered a position under Dr. Margaret Floosman in Wake Forest University's orthopedics department to research the wound-healing capacity of the human anterior cruciate ligament (ACL). By using the in situ hybridization technique, my colleagues and I determined that, contrary to the prevailing view, the ACL does not atrophy after being damaged but can potentially be repaired. This research work resulted in my first publication, in *Annals of Orthopedic Research*—and my commitment to a career in clinical medicine.

■ In 2008, I interned for the Little Rock Immunization Project, a Centers for Disease Control–funded study to determine why immunization rates in central Arkansas are disproportionately low. By interviewing anxious mothers in Little Rock emergency departments and overcoming daily cultural barriers to effective dialogue, I clarified for myself the role that socioeconomic factors play even in such seemingly simple procedures as pediatric immunizations. Skeptically, I learned how to transform extended, passionate discussions into mere boxes on our Excel spreadsheets. Together with the other observations gleaned in our five-year study, my data will be incorporated into recommendations that may help shape child health policy. But one question remains unanswered: how will our policy recommendations, which may not get implemented for another decade, ensure that the children whose mothers I interviewed are protected against polio and other infectious illnesses?

- As a research technician at the Zemlinsky Comprehensive Cancer Center at Case Western Reserve University, my primary role was to coordinate a clinical study to monitor salivary hormone levels in women trying to conceive. Suddenly, I was at the cutting edge of biomedical research and technology, and for the first time I had an opportunity to "teach" science by helping the study participants better understand their bodies. As a bonus, this past May the data from my study were published in *Women's Health Science*, and another paper I contributed will be published early next year. Today, I am doing an internship as a clinical research associate at Abbott Laboratories, where I have had to quickly learn the complexities of developing and executing pharmaceutical clinical trials. The issues surrounding the design of a cancer chemoprevention trial have become the subject of my master's thesis, which has required me to integrate the disciplines of basic science research, statistics, epidemiology, and pharmacoeconomics.

- In my sophomore year in college I was accepted into an undergraduate research program at the University of Maryland, College Park, which enabled me to work on an unusual research project with my genetics instructor, Dr. Bela Kodaly. The first assignment

Dr. Kodaly gave me was to sequence my own DNA! After only two days' work I was actually able to gaze down at the very sequence that defines me as a human being. That was only a taste of what was to come, however. Over the next nine weeks I worked on the genetic analysis of Canada geese, tanner crabs, and finally Inuits. In the Inuit project I analyzed mitochondrial DNA from Inuit groups across eastern Russia and North America. By evaluating and comparing a hypervariable portion of each group's mitochondrial DNA, we sought to establish their original migration patterns into North America as well as links between genetically similar Inuit populations. As a Canadian, I have always appreciated the diversity of the native cultures that surround me, so I was particularly excited to have an opportunity to help further Native Americans' knowledge of their history and heritage. The genetic history of entire peoples is only now beginning to be explored, and I am thrilled to have been a part of advancing our understanding in new ways.

- It's in keeping with my emphasis on the human benefits of research that most of my research breakthroughs have occurred at the intersection of clinical medicine and the lab—that is, in learning environments outside the classroom. My research into sleep and immune-mediating substances began as a direct result of observing patients. As an undergraduate summer student at the University of Miami Center for Sleep and Chronobiology, I was intrigued by the fact that patients who are sleep-deprived often complain not only of tiredness and fatigue but of frequent colds and flus. Is there a link between the immune system and sleep? These "extracurricular" observations sparked my research into the neural actions of substances that are both immune-enhancing and sleep-inducing. In fact, most if not all of my career accomplishments have grown out of just these kinds of informal learning situations. At international sleep conferences, for example, it was often the informal conversations that generated the best results and led to my collaborations with professors from the Universities of Chicago and Rochester. As I contemplate a career researching the intersection of sleep and immunology, I hope to leverage such informal learning to explore the ethical and social dimensions of my research. For example, because the causes of many mental diseases are unknown, many patients with debilitating problems are stigmatized by society. In Canada, for example, chronic fatigue syndrome was recognized as an illness only within the past decade. Before this, many patients were denied workers' compensation because there was no clear biochemical marker for their disease. As an MD/Ph.D. I will dedicate myself to uncovering the underlying pathologies of these mental health–related diseases.

■ Since last year I have been conceptualizing a new therapeutic strategy to treat stuttering using gamma-aminobutyric acid (GABA) modulators. Based on published neurochemical and psychiatric research, I concluded that GABAergic compounds could offer an effective therapy. I am currently working with the Stuttering Research Group at the London University Medical Center to draft, on my suggestion, a proposal for a clinical study of a specific GABAergic epilepsy drug in stutterers. My hope is that this potential therapeutic strategy will help stutterers like my brother, Minglie, become more fluent and thus better able to lead more productive and peaceful lives.

■ After graduating from Yale, I began researching sickle cell disease with Dr. Ferdinand Balboa and his colleagues at Washington Heights Children's Hospital and Research Center in New York City. I performed comprehensive chart reviews for every patient, created a detailed database, and learned how to read Pulmonary Function Tests and echocardiograms. My database revealed a disturbing pattern. By analyzing every available echo, I noticed that many sickle cell patients had pulmonary hypertension (PHT), though the cardiologist was not detecting it in the echoes. Moreover, some who were at high risk for PHT were not even being given the echo at all. The combination of sickle cell and PHT is often a death sentence, giving patients only two years to live. I shared my discovery with Dr. Balboa, and as a result plans are now underway to set up an echocardiogram clinic at the hospital. Because of the quality and extent of my data (which included pediatric patients), I was asked to present my data at the April 2008 Canadian Sickle Cell Symposium. Moreover, my research has culminated in my coauthorship of a paper for the *Journal of Pulmonary Science* on the statistically significant issues behind PHT and sickle cell disease.

■ Once I was at Brigham Young, I decided to pursue a dual major in biomedical and electrical engineering because I'm fascinated by the way engineering principles can be used to understand the human body. Biomedical instrumentation, research, and design classes showed me how the body's functioning can be measured, converted into signals, and processed to yield useful diagnostic data. I became excited by the way this technology is transforming medicine. Take tissue engineering. As a BYU Fellow,

I have been helping to generate viable cardiac tissue patches for implantation over or in place of damaged cardiac tissue. By optimizing the staining of multiple membrane proteins and creating a dye transfer protocol, I will be able to observe intercellular communication between host cardiac and potential implantation cell types to determine how closely the cell types couple. Electrocardiology is still another area that integrates biological and engineering techniques. In Professor Dunleavy's class I built an ECG circuit to measure the signal and output a voltage and also wrote a LabVIEW program to process, analyze, and output the signal. In doing so, I learned about the ECG's circuitry and signal processing and how the measured electrical signal's propagation through the heart corresponds to specific physical actions. I have also been able to explore electrocardiology through the Heart Health Center team at Brigham Young Medical College. My team (which I will lead next year as project manager) is working to transform the ECG into a wireless device that can measure the ECG signal and send it to a processing base. I'm excited by the practical impact of improving the circuit design's efficiency to reduce the device's size and verifying the robustness and accuracy of the wireless signal. Finally, my summer research at the University of Utah's

Stottlemyre Center for Proteomic Cell Signaling has enabled me to use proteasome extraction and DNA plasmid science to study myocardial infarctions at the cellular level.

- I was first exposed to laboratory research when I took a position in Novus Research's molecular biology department in 2007. Novus's high-throughput, in vivo mammalian "knockout" technology enabled us to identify and validate novel genomic drug targets at an extraordinary scale and speed. I especially enjoyed the laboratory design that allowed us to work together in small, tightly knit groups. I was invited to join the Exceptional Targets team, which met weekly to discuss methods to resolve the challenging gene targets that frequently provide the most interesting phenotype and biological insights. Meeting with scientists and group leaders helped me to better understand the molecular principles and logistics behind creating and characterizing "knockout" mice. Working today in Dr. Bryan Enders's lab at the Mayo Clinic, I have gained the opportunity to be at the forefront of immunology research. Using proteomic technologies, we are characterizing the serum of patients with autoimmune diseases such as rheumatoid arthritis (RA) and multiple sclerosis. One of our projects is to utilize these technologies to profile antibodies, cytokines, and other biomolecules in order to identify molecular fingerprints that will enable us to predict the responsiveness of RA patients to anti-TNF-alpha therapy. In the coming years, the practice of medicine will increasingly incorporate pharmacogenomic biomarkers such as HER2 for selecting breast cancer patients for treatment with Herceptin and, if our efforts are successful, pharmacoproteomic biomarkers to guide anti-TNF-alpha therapy. In the emerging era of personalized medicine, my background, knowledge, and experience will uniquely enable me to apply and interpret such tests as a physician.

■ Peering through a jar of wooden tongue depressors, Conner smiled and with a throaty gurgle asked "What's this?" An inquisitive, scrawny seven-year-old, Conner looked like any other normal kid at first glance. But to my fellow researchers at the Brown University Center for Pediatric Research, the small white circular object protruding from his neck told a different story. When I first learned of Conner's illness, "Ondines Curse," it sounded like something out of a bad Hollywood movie, but I quickly learned that Ondines is real and is most definitely a curse. According to Greek mythology, if a mortal fell in love with an Ondine, a beautiful mermaid-like creature, he was forever cursed to choose between sleep and breathing. Like those mortals, Conner lacked the ability to breath automatically. When he was awake, he could will himself to breathe, but when he fell asleep his breathing stopped. As a result, Conner was outfitted through an aperture in his neck with a ventilator that breathed for him while he slept. In earlier times infants with Ondines Curse would almost certainly have died shortly after birth. While today's patients can survive, they live limited lives. For no ventilator can pace breathing perfectly, and as a result many Ondines patients suffer brain damage caused by inadequate respiration.

Chapter 6 Perfect Phrases for Showing Thoughtfulness about Medicine

"In your opinion, what contemporary medical issue needs to be addressed in the U.S. healthcare system and why?"
(State University of New York, Stony Brook)

"What do you see as the most significant issue the medical profession will face in the next forty years?"
(University of Connecticut)

Earning double-digit MCAT scores and high grades in premed classes are two excellent ways to show that you have what it takes to go into medicine. But another is to show that you've thought seriously and deeply about the problems that confront the profession you claim to want to join. Application essays in which you thoughtfully analyze a medical issue or show you understand medicine's "bigger picture" can set you apart from the thousands of other applicants who focus only on their clinical experiences and burning desire to help others. Here are some perfect phrases illustrating applicants' thoughtfulness about medicine.

- The experience in hospital finance I gained at Medical College of Wisconsin afforded me a behind-the-scenes look at the business side of medicine. Counseling patients and families on the costs of their proposed treatments drove home for me the human impact of medicine's high costs. Some patients were denied care, while others were forced to take on unimaginable debt. As I worked to improve collection rates, cut costs, and optimize patient billing, I saw how revenue pressures are forcing health care's practitioners to demand that more patients be scheduled at the same time that clinic expenses are cut further.

- My research on income inequality at the National Poverty Research Council proved beyond all doubt to me that increasing medical access for the uninsured has implications far beyond just preventing illness. It reduces income inequality and economic dependency by increasing individuals' capacity for work and thus their ability to improve their situation. In a very real sense, by becoming a physician and providing medical care to the uninsured, I will be able to help my patients break the poverty cycle by giving them the health they need to pursue education and better careers.

- Today, I consult at Phoenix-area medical centers. As part of a team of consultants for SunCare, I worry that the federal government's Medicare Ambulatory Payment Classification System will adversely affect our hospitals' already precarious finances. Instead of interviewing mothers, I interview charge nurses, attending physicians, registration clerks, and department managers to target opportunities for missed reimbursements. Based on our quantitative analyses, we issue recommendations to improve department-specific accuracy, hospitalwide efficiency, and federal regulatory compliance. But how can analyzing Medicare reimbursements address the even greater public health issues that our nation faces?

- My ambition to help people by practicing medicine was reaffirmed when I participated in the Tulane pain rounds last fall. The weekly rounds at New Orleans General Hospital were attended by a group of physicians, surgeons, psychologists, physical therapists, and researchers who collaborated to examine the most enigmatic of pain cases. Although there were rarely simple solutions for these debilitated patients, I learned that a multidisciplinary approach to pain management can provide insights that would otherwise be unavailable to each specialization individually. My participation in the pain rounds opened my eyes to the complexities of clinical decision making. With this firsthand exposure to the

➡

hospital setting and the expertise of medical professionals, my decision to pursue a medical career was sealed.

■ Last year I was a tutor for Kansas City People Advocates, whose sponsoring company, a neighborhood development corporation, offers subsidized health care to low-income families. I was stunned to discover that the subsidized health care this corporation offers goes sorely underutilized. In conversations with parents I learned that cultural biases—including a belief in showing silent strength in the face of hardship—often restrain Hispanic mothers from seeking preventive health care for their kids. Clearly, providing low-cost insurance and accessible, multilingual health clinics for immigrant children is only part of an effective health-care solution. Equally important is ensuring that the health-care clinics and local health programs meet a high quality standard that encourages people to walk through clinic doors, while still respecting their cultural views about health care. Finally, my tutoring in Kansas City's Hispanic community has also taught me that low academic performance can be directly attributable to students' health. Colds, flus, and even tuberculosis go unchecked by hardworking immigrant parents who work long hours and who, because of language barriers and low education levels, are unaware of the importance of regular doctors' visits.

■ "There is a body of knowledge peculiar to the medical problems and needs of military units, and that knowledge base is different from that required in ordinary medical practice." As a youngster watching war movies made painfully real by the vivid commentary of my late uncle, a World War II veteran, I knew that military medicine was, in Dr. James Zimble's words, "different" from conventional medicine, especially in combat casualty care. It was in a college philosophy course, "Morality and War," at Auburn University, however, that I first began to seriously grapple with the issues peculiar to military medicine. In discussing the notions of morality and justice in the context of combat, Professor Ian Powys forced us to compare the unsentimentally pragmatic ethics of the soldier and medic in battle to the more abstract and less urgent morality of civilian practitioners. Clearly, the military physician is sometimes torn between his or her duty to the Hippocratic oath and duty to the military in such areas as patient privacy, the ethics of withholding treatment to extract information from a POW, and determining what behavior is "moral" in combat situations. I am drawn to a military medical career because the ethical

➥

issues unique to it will only grow as the U.S. military faces such emerging challenges as coping with extended worldwide deployments, its growing humanitarian role during natural disasters, and the steadily increasing population of military retirees.

■ My intellectual interest is Buddhist psychology, which I believe can be linked to medicine. Buddhism's goal is to end suffering for all through the Four Noble Truths, which essentially teach individuals to live a life that benefits everyone in such a way that any individual can be happy without possessing anything. Though in our materialistic society this is obviously a difficult ideal to live up to, I believe we can each work to end suffering in our own individual ways. As I took courses in Buddhism and premed subjects at Cornell, I began to see that as a physician I could work to alleviate patients' mental suffering just as much as their physical pain. As a volunteer with the Health Staff Assistant Program and the Ithaca Cardiac Clinic, I saw that, quite aside from their medical skills, the attitude, philosophy, and manner that doctors bring to bear on each patient can create a positive and tangible effect in patients that can reduce suffering and save lives.

■ I believe that it is as a physician that I can best address the urgent health-care issues the United States faces today. Take home hospice care. Today, the Delaware

Hospice of Dover serves more people each year than any other in the mid-Atlantic states, and most of Kent County's foreseeable deaths are serviced by the hospice. This is a direct result of the determined fund-raising efforts of the hospice's administration, many of its volunteers, and residents of Dover, but also of the effective education that the hospice gives its volunteers, who often have no idea what a hospice does before enrolling in the program. Last August, after learning about the Delaware Hospice, I began volunteering weekly in its clinic. The patients I have helped have genuinely benefited because of the emotional reassurance and controlled pain management I provide. This is the kind of medicine that attracts me—efficient systems that serve diverse people's needs and operate effectively while staying close to their communities.

■ As a child growing up in Bosnia, my life was harshly interrupted by the devastating Yugoslav wars of the 1990s. The bombing of cities, including my own, Citluk, was a frequent occurrence. My older brother, Andro, and I served as volunteer EMTs for three years, and together we witnessed the horrors of war and genocide. By the time I was only 16, the sight of blood and death had quite ceased to shock me. After each explosion, the survivors, including myself, would routinely head out into the streets and alleys to methodically pull the victims out of their shattered homes. Because there weren't enough (and in some instances, any) medical emergency vehicles, we loaded many victims onto the back of dusty pickup trucks for the trip to the local hospitals, whose primitive sterilization techniques sometimes cost victims their lives. All around me I saw dramatic evidence of what medical attention—of even the most rudimentary kind—can mean to people in need.

- When I was traveling through the Philippines, I observed a shocking reality that contradicted my parents' romanticized picture of my "homeland." Almost everywhere I traveled, I saw rural youth addicted to opium. In village after village, I saw the same blank stares and bulging eyes. Despite a massive influx of opium from Thailand and Laos, government officials paid only lip service to curbing opium trafficking at best and at worst actively supplied the drug, especially during election time. Though I had planned to stay in Manila only six weeks, I remained over a year. Armed with a few papers from the Internet, a *Physician Assistant's Drug Handbook,* and Peiser and Sandry's *The Universal 12-Step Program*, I set out with the modest ambition of changing the world. Sleeping with rodent-sized insects, showering with wild toads, and digging holes in the hard ground for toilets were not what made these months so challenging. It was the sheer magnitude of the Philippines' drug problem. In Manila, unlike the United States, drug addiction is seen as a moral vice rather than an illness. Rehabilitation facilities are scarce, and few families wish to acknowledge the problem for fear of public shame. Despite these daunting obstacles and my at best shaky command of Tagalog, I felt for the first time in my life that I had a calling.

- I have spent hundreds of hours volunteering in clinical health-care settings—Johns Hopkins Hospital and Chestertown Health Center and, since 2008, Nashville Municipal Hospital's emergency room. Today, I transport patients, deliver lab specimens, clean and prepare patient rooms, and talk with patients to make them feel comfortable—all in the same environment that was so intimidating to me as an eight-year-old. I have seen residents literally work entire days without taking a break to eat. I have seen on-call physicians forced to leave weddings to come to the ER, or in some cases left with no choice but to drag their children to the hospital with them. And beyond these personal sacrifices, I have also seen the unfortunate truth that doctors cannot always honestly reassure patients and their loved ones that everything will be

➡

all right. For example, my uncle Roy, ravaged by tongue cancer, was initially treated with chemotherapy, but it eventually failed. His doctors then surgically removed his larynx, but the cancer still spread. Losing him after an eight-year battle will always be a grim personal reminder of the limits of modern medicine. And yet nothing of what I've witnessed has diminished the awe I still feel at doctors' power to save lives and comfort patients.

- The anxious hospital scene before me aroused the same sense of injustice I had felt only a year before when California passed the anti-immigrant Proposition 187 and over a million people—400,000 kids—were suddenly denied basic medical care. As a high school student, I had helped organize a student protest at UC San Diego, collecting over 500 signatures to overturn the new law. As the daughter of two immigrants, I was raised to revere the ideals of equality and opportunity, so when I began to define what "equality" meant to me, I saw health care as a fundamental component. Everyone deserves a fair shot at a healthy, productive life.

- Evaluating my health-related involvements on a social scale—by the extent to which I have been able to provide care directly to those who most need it—has accelerated my personal route to the profession of medicine. As a physician in a large, urban hospital, I might be able to safeguard Angel's T-cell count. I could immunize disenfranchised children and increase their access to health care. I could incorporate my understanding of the emotional consequences of HIV infection with concrete, clinical knowledge. And I could lead fellow physicians, with my growing understanding of methods for improving hospital efficiency, in efforts to reform health policy. I am eager to do all this, yet I realize that medicine will still ask even more profound questions of me: Can the necessary efficiencies that a market-driven health-care system provides exist in a more publicly managed, universal health-care system? Can I reconcile my idealism with the reality of health-care finances today?

■ I concur with Carl Elliot's observation that medicine's greatest philosophical problems are not caused by institutional or technological developments but by perplexities arising from the very nature and ends of medicine. For example, although the physicians at United Care found our health assessment tool to be a useful initial intake health screen, they did not accept it as the gold standard for comprehensive care as we had hoped. I believe physician and bioethicist John Lantos has explained why we failed: medicine cannot effectively evaluate itself because it

➡

cannot agree on what the criteria for that self-evaluation should be.

- The three weeks I spent as my ailing grandmother's nurse aide in a Pakistani hospital will stay with me until I die. Pakistan's chronic shortage of medical staff and funding shifts the burden for providing care squarely onto the family, even when a patient has been hospitalized. Although I took on this responsibility gladly for my grandmother, I was saddened by Rawalpindi City Hospital's old, poorly maintained facility and equipment, the appalling ratio of patients to staff, and the doctors' complete eschewal of anything like a "bedside manner." In many cases, doctors were downright rude to patients. Even simple hygiene such as hand-washing was dispensed with. In those few weeks, my determination to become the kind of doctor who could help patients like my grandmother grew in intensity and focus.

- Learning, dedication, and compassion are the tools of physicians and teachers alike. As an intern at Ohio University Medical Center and at Boone Clinic in Cincinnati, I watched as doctors used all three of these skills to help patients maintain good mental, physical, and spiritual health. If patients were healthy, they taught them how to stay that way. If patients were ill, they taught them how to become better. I remember watching a grin grow across a father's face as Dr. Hume taught him about nerves and how they slowly grow back after certain injuries. The man was relieved to learn that his daughter would soon regain feeling in her fingers. It is this principle element of a doctor's job—healing through teaching—that is perhaps the primary reason I am so strongly driven to a career in medicine.

Chapter 7 Perfect Phrases for Describing Your Journey to Medicine

"How did you reach your decision to enter medicine?"

(Loyola University Chicago)

Knowing that you want to go to medical school and what you want to do afterward are not enough by themselves to produce an effective medical school application essay. For many applicants, describing the life experiences that brought them to the decision to become a doctor will be essential essay topics. This is especially true for nontraditional applicants who need to convince the admissions committee that their reasons for waiting to attend medical school are compelling ones. Poor "journey-to-medicine" essays try to convince the committee that the applicant has "always" wanted to become a doctor or that medicine is somehow his manifest destiny because his parent was a physician or because the applicant was good at science. Good journey-to-medicine essays, in contrast, tell a vivid, detailed, real story, in which the applicant gradually becomes aware that medical school is the best use of her talents and passions. In other words, the difference between credible and incredible journey-to-medicine essays is a matter of honesty, reflection, specificity, and personality.

- Despite my success at Bain and the intellectual challenge of my work, management consulting cannot offer me the kind of exhilaration I discovered when I mentored college students for my church and provided clinical care to Hudson Valley Hospital's patients. My mind has returned to medicine—this time of its own accord. Medicine offers me intellectual rigor, real and dramatic human impact, and even perhaps the potential to shape health policy.

- Juvenile corrections is just one of many environments in which I have applied my skills as a psychiatric nurse treating underserved populations. Over the past four years I have honed my clinical skills with hundreds of patients from every demographic population, and have adapted successfully to diverse practice settings. Because of my experience in the clinical trenches, my decision to become a physician is based not on glorified notions but on a hard-earned understanding of the long hours and difficult decisions this calling requires. My patients have taught me a lot, expanded my definition of compassion, and given meaning to my daily work. The empathy I feel when I provide psychiatric care to abused children at the Cook County Children's Home, the pride I feel when an inner-city schoolchild I am treating begins to succeed academically, the satisfaction I know when a patient with developmental delays (whose grandmother calls him "little Rain Man") plays little league baseball for the first time—these emotions, elicited by literally hundreds of underprivileged patients, are the reward for my long hectic days providing patient care.

■ My legal education has given me the maturity, self-discipline, and tenacity I need to excel in medical school. Perhaps more importantly, reading and evaluating disability and tort cases have made me acutely aware of the significance of doctors' impacts on their patients' lives. A single mishap can cost patients not just their health, but also in some cases their quality of life, livelihood, and ability to contribute to society. Law school may have cost me time, but it also made me acutely aware of the responsibilities of a physician. As such, I am now prepared to undertake this career path not just with excitement, but with the utmost sense of purpose.

■ My desire to help the sick became a reality when my family fled to Cambodia in 1994. There, we were placed in a refugee camp strictly fenced and patrolled

➡

by Cambodian guards. Though the conditions were oppressive, crowded, and unclean, I made the most of the limited opportunities and, still only 10, began working in the primitive and cramped hospital as a nurse. After intensively studying English so I could translate between the patients and the Western doctors, I began taking vital signs, administering and monitoring medications, and cleaning up and stitching wounds. I saw with dramatic force that while science is the basis of medicine, humanity and compassion are its soul. I decided then to become a physician.

- I don't regret my extended "temporary" chemistry career in the least. It has allowed me to learn a tremendous amount about the pharmaceutical industry and about the science that underlies medicine. It has also given me a chance to mature and, in doing so, to realize that I still have the same ambition I did when I was 12 years old: to be a doctor. In my career I've experienced the manufacturing and testing side of the pharmaceuticals that doctors prescribe to patients every day. Now I want to benefit those patients directly as their physician.

- Was it possible that I could adjust from veterinary medicine to the realities and challenges of human medicine? To test this, I began volunteering at

Oklahoma Veterans Hospital through the Veterans of Foreign Wars. The benefits of working in a veterans hospital were greater than I could have imagined. The doctors and medical technicians, and especially the technician Cindy Zhang, taught me how to read X-rays and how to set casts. The technicians and nurses let me interview patients and obtain their medical histories. After more than 104 hours of exposure to common illnesses, diabetes, allergy reactions, orthopedic injuries, and pain in every variety, I began to see more and more links between what I had seen in the veterinary clinic and what I was witnessing in the hospital wards. But there was also one major difference: investing myself in other people through human medicine was more exciting, personal, and rewarding.

■ My parents always wanted me to become a doctor. I never disagreed when they told me that medicine was the most "respectable," even the noblest, of the professions, but I didn't want to follow a career path that had already been chosen for me—I wanted to discover it for myself. I have always loved the sciences, especially chemistry. In fact, at Caltech the first class I registered for was organic chemistry. Fascinated by the problem-solving nature of the subject, I decided that chemistry was the profession for me. In a

➡

biochem lab my freshman year I learned valuable skills and techniques while helping a postdoctoral student with her project, and by the next year I was running my own project in an orgo lab. However, I was also realizing that discussing chem research with peers and professors didn't provide me with sufficient people contact. For all its compensations, research wasn't enough. I wanted to be able to see directly how my actions were useful to others.

■ I was surprised by how deeply the ER experience affected me. The laboratory research I was doing no longer seemed as critical, and I began to identify with the teamwork in the ER more than with the isolating nature of my bench work. I also began to see that clinical medicine could provide an unparalleled opportunity to use scientific knowledge in an exciting, high-impact way. Since then, my road back to medicine has been reinforced by experiences, including the suicide of a close friend, that have shown me how important it is that I have a career that affects people's lives.

■ Sometimes it takes tragedy to turn your life around. For me it was the death of my cousin Courtney in my senior year of college. Before Courtney's death I had been spinning my wheels academically; I didn't know what I wanted to do, and my lack of focus and

25-hour-a-week job played a big part in my lack of academic success. Courtney was older and more worldly than me and had an amazing energy about her that made me enthusiastic about whatever topic she talked about. Her sudden death from lung cancer severely affected me and sparked my desire to learn more about this plague. As I tried to finish my double major in physics and Russian, I took my first classes in biology and found myself energized by the field of molecular biology.

■ Today as a pharmacist for MedsPlus Pharmacy I have the opportunity to see firsthand how the health-care system affects people's lives. I have comforted young mothers who were unsure of the brand-new steps they were taking, offered my understanding to relatives of cancer patients who came to pick up medications, and listened compassionately as customers told me they were forced to choose between buying food and paying for their medications. I chose to practice as a pharmacist in the community rather than in a hospital or home health setting because I knew the constant interaction with people would help prepare me for my medical career. As a pharmacist I have gained experience by not simply filling prescriptions but by actually caring for people, understanding their health environment, and

➡

learning more about what I need to do to strengthen my ability to help others.

- As a child, I didn't fear visits to the doctor's office. I looked forward to them. They were a chance to escape to a clean, orderly world where anxiety and illness were magically turned into reassurance and health. Medicine had an element of mystery about it. When I was about 10, my mother became pregnant with my baby brother. I was old enough to understand that there was another human being inside of my mother's body and became fascinated by the human body and, specifically, the reproductive system. I began to imagine what it would be like to hold in your hands the power and trust to safeguard people's health.

- The sheer number of classmates who apparently knew they were destined for a career in medicine startled me. To me, medicine had always seemed like a natural progression from my high school career, where I had excelled academically, volunteered in a hospital, and conducted research. University would be only a stepping-stone to my ultimate destination. Now with every raised hand in Professor Ott's "Career Planning" class I saw that medical school was a natural aspiration for a great many of my peers as well. It was precisely their certainty that first made me seriously question my own desire to become a doctor. I realized that the decision to study medicine requires more than the feeling that it is a "natural" career choice. It requires careful examination of one's motives, an understanding of the real demands of the career, and, most importantly, the certainty that one has chosen the correct career above all alternatives.

- When I was 13, my grandmother died of lung cancer. I had a close, loving relationship with her and felt helpless as she suffered through the disease. My grandmother was a chain smoker, and her death taught me the importance of healthy living. As a teenager, I sought to pass these values on to others and worked at health fairs teaching children about the dangers of smoking and the importance of nutrition and exercise. Two years into a successful career in advertising, I joined a team focused on promoting the Marlboro cigarette brand to Chinese women. At first, I attacked the project with the same industriousness I had brought to my other work at the agency, but I soon felt pangs of apprehension. My grandmother had died of lung cancer, and I was helping a tobacco company sell cigarettes? Late one night, as I worked on a demographic profile of Marlboro's "target" customer, I finally realized I had had enough. A month later I left the ad business and focused full time on pursuing a career in medicine.

■ When I was growing up, my parents and I were always volunteering—distributing groceries at food banks, getting out the vote for local candidates, helping fellow Muslim immigrants in Toronto. But, in addition to such "extracurricular" giving, my parents showed me how much more can be accomplished when that giving is your career. My father's work in municipal finance enables cities to fund hospitals and schools; my mother, a planner for the City of Buffalo, oversees the creation of housing for low-income families.

My parents' deep satisfaction with the public service thrust of their jobs set a profound example for me. When I finally realized that becoming a physician was the perfect expression of my own desire for public service, I began pursuing my calling with gusto.

I commuted over 100 miles a day four times a week to earn a life sciences degree at the University of Virginia. I also learned more about medicine while serving as a volunteer coordinator of a program to train physicians at a level-one trauma center in St. Louis's Riverside Medical Center. This was an extraordinary program that integrated a tremendous teaching experience into the very eclectic milieu of a major metropolitan inner-city environment. At Riverside Medical Center I learned that there is an acute need for committed and compassionate doctors who possess a keen sense

➡

of community and who can establish trust with their patients regardless of the circumstances that caused them to seek treatment.

- In June 2005, I had the opportunity to attend the North American Youth Leadership Forum on Medicine in Washington, DC, after my physics teacher recommended me to the program. For 10 days, 325 students from the United States, Canada, and Mexico came together to learn about the current state of medicine. From trips to the National Institutes of Health and daylong discussions about HIV/AIDS to lectures by Dr. Pablo Vironez (director of the Vaccines and Immunization Program at the South American Health Organization) and Dr. Patch Adams (the same man depicted in the Robin Williams movie), we explored many of the issues that shape medicine today and will influence my career as a physician and caregiver for years to come.

- My fascination with the complexities of the human body and the rapid technological advances in the war against disease inspired me to major in medical technology at Emory University. I hoped my first job, as a medical technologist with Saint Andrews Hospital in Biloxi, Mississippi, would bring me the sense of fulfillment I longed for. But though I learned a lot about hematology, urinalysis, microbiology, and

➡

medical instruments and procedures, I became increasingly disappointed with my strictly behind-the-scenes role. At every opportunity I crept down to the emergency room to put a face to the specimen I tested. I enthusiastically made rounds with phlebotomists and found out how much I enjoyed holding the hand of a child or elderly patient or just offering him or her a friendly smile. Believing I could more directly serve the community in a public health role, I obtained my master's degree in public health in 2006 and joined the Biloxi Department of Public Health. My experiences there and with the patients at Saint Andrews showed me that public health could involve much more than just inspecting homes and educating people about lead poisoning. Feeling inexorably driven toward medical school, I enrolled at the University of Mississippi's postbaccalaureate premed program in 2007.

- Back in Croatia I began looking for opportunities to learn English, and in 2001 I spent 10 months in London studying the language. Upon graduating, I enrolled in the physical therapy program at the Royal Academy of Physical Education. But when I began studying the clinical sciences and, for the first time, had direct contact with patients and health-care staff, I realized that I wanted to extend my knowledge of medicine and the human body beyond the physical therapy curriculum. I also realized that I wanted a level of responsibility and patient interaction that only physicians possess. I decided then that after earning my diploma in physical therapy, I would apply to medical school.

Chapter 8 Perfect "Why Medicine?" Phrases

"Describe your motivation to become a physician."

(University of Connecticut)

"Describe your motivation for a career in medicine and experiences you have had that helped confirm this desire."

(Ohio State University)

The perfect phrases In the last chapter describe the autobiographical path or personal journey that led applicants toward medicine. This chapter focuses on the next step in that process: applicants' direct statements of their reasons for choosing a medical career. All the following perfect phrases show the applicants "cutting to the chase" and declaring exactly what it is that draws them to the physicians' calling. Let the internal logic and flow of your essay guide you in determining where exactly this "theme" statement belongs in your essay.

- Although I cannot predict how I will react to death, I do know how I react to life. One day as I walked into an examination room, I felt a tug on my lab coat. A young girl, recovered from food poisoning and brimming with energy, decided to give me a tour of her room—from the tables to the sink. The joy I saw on her face was priceless. Once pale and weak, she was healthy and could play again! Participating in this rejuvenation of hope and energy is what I want to achieve as a physician. I cannot honestly imagine a better, more deeply satisfying way to live my life.

- As part of Hope Hospital's medical team, I passed out condoms, distributed needle-sterilizing bleach, and measured the blood pressure of the homeless in Union Square. As I worked my way through the needy gathered across the park, I realized that even as a volunteer, my small medical contribution could make a tremendous difference if it protected even one of them from contracting the AIDS virus. This was a humbling and exhilarating moment for me. And this remains the way I view a physician's impact: a doctor's help and compassion may not greatly affect everyone, but for a few patients it can make all the difference in the world.

- My most dramatic exposure to the physician's power to heal came last year when an injured window washer was brought into the emergency room.

He had fallen off some scaffolding and struck his unprotected head against the concrete. His cries of pain and agonized writhing under his restraints still echo in my mind. As I stepped toward the bed to help the nurses and doctors, I looked into the man's eyes and burned with frustration at my powerlessness to help him. I later learned that a CT scan had revealed a bulge of blood pressing against the man's brain, causing his acute head and eye pain. Surgeons performed risky surgery to drain the excess blood from beneath his skull. Later that week, a smiling window washer returned to the emergency room and proceeded to personally thank everyone with a hug. I want to become a physician because no other profession bestows this same awesome responsibility or emotional compensation.

- One look into Evelina's sad eyes convinced me that a doctor's greatest responsibility is to be a caregiver, not simply a medical provider. One never just treats a patient—one treats a person. In the process, one also "treats" all those close to him or her—people who are often disheartened, confused, frightened, and frustrated. By understanding now how physical healing must be complemented by emotional support, I have strived to provide this total care in all my interactions in the ward. Medicine is the best way for me to serve and express the compassion I was raised with while also challenging me at the highest intellectual, physical, and spiritual levels.

- One reason I have chosen to pursue a career in military medicine is the broad patient population I will encounter, one that is actually broader than physicians find in most civilian environments. My cousin, Dr. Chin-Hwa Seong, a physician and nephrologist for the Air Force Hospital in Seoul, explained to me that what he enjoys most about military medicine is the opportunity to treat both the healthy and physically fit—the personnel of the Korean Air Force—as well as a broader universe of patients—the flyers' families and civilians. Chin-Hwa helped me understand that as a military physician I can experience this diversity and that it will help to prepare me for the greater diversity I will encounter if I am deployed to underserved or to refugee areas overseas. Moreover, my extensive background in biotechnology may be an asset as the military copes with the special threats of bioterrorism. Finally, I am drawn to military medicine because I believe it rewards leadership. Leadership takes many forms, and only one of them is where you sit in the chain of command.

- From the day I saw Dr. Stadelman cheat death in an emergency room to my moving experiences at

Kalamazoo Free Clinic I have witnessed the different ways that physicians can use their time to protect life. Whether they practice in an ER or a family clinic, they must be assertive, cool, and decisive yet also caring, "heartful," and patient. I want to commit my time in life to embodying these qualities. Dr. Stadelman's life-saving actions were a vivid wake-up call to me that how we choose to spend our precious seconds in this life can have the most ultimate of impacts on others' lives. I too want to be the one who, instead of standing helplessly by, has the skill and cool to save a human life.

- Teaching, kindness, research, and learning are only a few of the essential tools of the physician's trade, but I will always believe they are the most important. Like no other profession, medicine offers something for my mind and my heart. Medicine simply seems the most direct and powerful way to help people, physically, emotionally, even spiritually. I have chosen osteopathic medicine over allopathic medicine because I believe hands-on manipulative treatment offers unique benefits in relieving pain, restoring range of motion, and enhancing the body's natural capacity to heal itself. Osteopathic medicine also seems to promote a stronger patient-doctor bond, and in my personal experience osteopaths are often more down-to-earth and compassionate physicians. Central California, where I intend to practice, is home to large, unassimilated Hmong and Mexican communities where allopathic medicine is viewed with distrust. As an osteopathic physician I will be able to "infiltrate" these communities and challenge the orthodoxy that effective medicine can be provided only in a designated health facility. By working with community leaders and organizing weekend health clinics in local parks and supermarket parking lots, I can help bring medicine to the most underserved.

■ I want to know that I am directly enabling people to enjoy better quality of living and a better chance at life. Instead of a "great day" meaning the occasional smooth-as-glass landing or extremely uneventful flight, I want to take home the relieved smile on my patients' faces or the look of gratitude in their eyes. I can think of no better way than becoming a physician to end each day knowing that I have helped someone with all my knowledge, all my skill, and all my commitment. Medicine is not just what I want to do, but who I want to be.

■ Three weeks later, an envelope arrived containing a thank-you card and a photo of me with the Martinez family. That gesture immediately reminded me of the gifts another couple had sent my physician father every Christmas for 10 years. They were showing the kind of gratitude and joy that no other profession I know of enables those who are privileged enough to practice it to see. In return for the chance to experience a lifetime of that kind of gratification, I intend to use my experience overcoming cultural and language barriers to bring better health care to America's new immigrant communities.

- In high school, I had a neighbor, Patrick, who, 300 pounds overweight and suffering from diabetes, heart disease, and arthritis, was confined to his home. On my visits to help him around the house, we would talk about his condition, and I would encourage him to practice healthy eating habits. Tragically, though he was aware of his risk factors, he didn't alter his behavior and died of a heart attack at age 35. I remember wondering—if I had been Patrick's physician, could I have saved his life? Could I have treated his conditions more effectively or convinced him to make better lifestyle choices? For me, curiosity—asking these difficult questions—and compassion—wanting to be the one who provides the answers—have led me to seek a medical career.

- I no longer think in idealistic terms of "changing the world" because I realize that helping a few individuals enjoy better health is a far more practical objective and, in the end, accomplishes the same goal in a more satisfyingly personal way. By becoming a physician, I can combine humane compassion and scientific methods to "change the world" one patient at a time.

- So why must I be a doctor? There are definitely other professions that serve communities' physical, mental, and emotional well-being. However, physicians are the only people I know of who have the skills and expertise to help people when they are most vulnerable: when their health is failing or at risk. Moreover, as a doctor, I can provide not only strong leadership within the medical community to other African Americans, but I can serve as a role model for underrepresented minorities considering medicine, thereby reflecting positively on my family and my community. By studying medicine and becoming a physician, I can offer society an advocate for quality medical care, provide poor communities with a guardian of good health, and give myself a lifetime of fulfillment.

- As Kearsage Health Center's phlebotomist, I am known throughout the hospital as the "friendly vampire" because I make it my goal to allay the fears of mothers in the labor and delivery ward, elderly patients in the cardiac intensive care unit, and needle-fearing children on the pediatrics floor. I try to bring this same selflessness to my medical teammates. When the trauma bells sound, I sprint through the hospital halls to the emergency room, where I come together with the doctor, ER techs, and trauma nurses in a moment of pure harmony to create a smooth symphony of precise coordinated action. More than anything, this attitude of "other-mindedness" has helped me cope with the emotional boom-and-bust of daily life at Kearsage, the desolate feeling when an innocent victim of drunk driving dies, and the exhilaration when a hopeless patient is brought back from the brink.

■ The intellectual challenges of research are satisfying, but the reward of patient interaction is what truly motivates me. During one of my conversations with Dr. Lindvegg, I asked him what drives him to work 20-hour days. He told me that the thrill of seeing patients like Mrs. Brett pull through difficult surgeries keeps him energized. But he also made sure I understood that not every patient can be helped. One day he asked me to accompany him as he informed a new patient, Olga, of the results of a standard medical screening. In a closet-sized room, I listened as Dr. Lindvegg told Olga that because of a tumor on the surface of her left lung, a pneumonectomy had to be performed immediately. We all knew that if it was malignant, the cancer would

➡

be too vigorous to stop. Being there as the 28-year-old mother of two confronted her own mortality was an intensely emotional moment for me. Within a month, the cancer took her life. Seeing Mrs. Brett's dramatic surgery on my first day of shadowing convinced me to become a physician, but it was the moment with Olga that made me realize why. The ramifications of a physician's actions are infinite. Whether the patient survives, like Mrs. Brett, or dies, like Olga, the physician has played perhaps the weightiest role of all—fighting for another's health and life.

- To me medicine represents the elegant balance of human interaction, social duty, and intellectual stimulation. I have chosen it as a career because I want to incorporate all three of these themes into my life and work. The medical field offers a wealth of opportunities for building a private practice, teaching, conducting basic or clinical research, and working in overseas health-care development. I don't want a career that forces me to choose between my love of social interaction, my intellectual interest in science, and my instinct toward public service. As a doctor, I won't have to.

- How have my health-care experiences affected my career goals? The idealistic answer would be to say that they have reaffirmed the romanticized view of medicine I held at age 13 when I watched my grandfather get sick and miraculously recover. However, they have also given me the opportunity to see the side of medicine that is not always so glamorous—the times at Peoria General when doctors cursed the fact that they hadn't seen their kids in days; the exasperation I felt when kids at the teen alcoholics clinic refused to listen to me even though they knew I told them the truth; the patients who complained that their medications weren't working and aimed accusatory fingers at their physicians. Despite these moments, medicine is one of the few fields that is centered almost completely around service, where a person can have the most tangible possible impact on others' lives every single day.

Chapter 9 Perfect Phrases for Goals

"Where do you see yourself in your medical career ten to fifteen years from now?"

(University of Alabama)

"Although interests may change, at the present time, in what field of medicine are you most interested?"

(Tulane University)

M edical schools do not expect applicants, especially those applying directly out of college, to provide a full-fledged post-MD career plan. However, if you do have some general sense of what areas of medicine appeal to you—such as an area of specialization, urban versus rural settings, or academic versus private practice—then the following perfect phrases may come in handy. Sometimes in general terms, sometimes quite specifically, the applicants in these examples scope out where they think their medical careers will take them.

- My hospital work enabled me to shadow a cardiologist and a gastroenterologist through their hospital rounds and office appointments. Because of this exposure to these specializations, my previous volunteer work in a pediatrician's office, and my experiences with pediatrics patients this summer, I am more confident than ever that my main focus should remain general pediatrics, a commitment that stems from my personal experience with my handicapped sister as well as my joy in working with children. After graduating from medical school, I plan to enter a program that provides physicians to underserved communities. I will then specialize in pediatrics and become a primary care physician. Making a difference in a child's life is especially rewarding because the benefits will last an entire lifetime. This is what draws me to a career in pediatrics, specifically one in an inner-city setting. Most realistically, I envision myself as a pediatrician in a large urban physicians group that is part of several preferred provider organization (PPO) networks and affiliated with a major hospital.

- My years of medical volunteerism and experiences watching my physician father struggle with his private practice have convinced me that tomorrow's successful physician must have a solid grasp of business practices and strong management skills. To gain these business skills, last year I became one of two third-year science department students (out of fifty-five applicants) selected for the University of Arizona's five-year dual-degree MBA/MD program. My understanding of the "big picture" of medicine today will enable me to be a resource to my fellow practitioners as they navigate the complexities of the managed-care marketplace and increasingly burdensome government health-care regulations. But a physician trained in management and business will also be better equipped to help his patients cope in the health-care marketplace. However, having the skills to manage one's practice effectively and efficiently should never cause the physician to lose sight of his primary responsibility—the individual patient.

■ Tragically, many clinics like Bird Rock Community Health are struggling because of fewer available grants and rising caseloads and malpractice insurance costs. Although U.S. hospitals can support emergency care for the poor, basic medical care is still a luxury for tens of millions, even in this country of plenty. By experiencing both medicine's public health challenges at the Sloan Institute for Public Health and the one-on-one relationships that are the heart of the physician's calling at Canton Health Center, I have refined my career goals as a physician: to be a doctor

➡

who is involved in the political dimension of medical delivery, serves the underserved, and educates her patients about the issues that affect their health.

■ Since observing Dr. Dravecky in action, I have been motivated by one driving goal—to become a surgeon. Last year, I took advantage of opportunities to view an appendectomy, cholecystectomy, and angioplasty as a member of Nebraska State's premedical society. Learning about surgery firsthand from plastic and orthopedic surgeons as an officer of the university's surgical interest group only fueled my passion. All these experiences have shown me that surgery is a demanding profession that requires dexterity, precision, stamina, and cool. It's a hands-on specialty that has an immediate and profound impact on patients. This is what appeals to me about surgery and assures me that I will thrive as a surgeon.

■ According to the United Nations study *Key Issues in World Health Care,* the elderly will account for 20 percent of the U.S. population by 2050. As a gerontologist affiliated with a major urban health center in Florida or Arizona, I can help treat the noncommunicable diseases that typically affect the elderly, from cancer and cardiovascular diseases to diabetes and Alzheimer's. Once or twice a week I will donate my time to a free clinic like the Senior

➡

Community Clinic of El Paso, where I now volunteer weekends and holidays alongside the clinic's two volunteer doctors. Becoming a gerontologist will enable me to provide a higher, more complex level of care to my patients, to address both their primary medical care and emotional needs, and to practice in a population where I can maximize my impact.

- My ultimate career goal is to empower communities like Camden to take charge of their children's' long-term health via preventive medicine and health education. Learning the basic etiology of the diseases prevalent in such underserved communities is crucial to developing health education solutions that effectively halt diseases and disorders early in their formation. The most effective way for me to understand these community-specific disorders and their etiology is to attend medical school and then establish a practice in these underserved communities. Later in my career, I hope to also use my JD degree to identify higher-level mechanisms for implementing the preemptive health-care methods I develop as a medical practitioner, perhaps by working with organizations like the NIH's Office of Minority Health.

- That special relationship I saw between the internist and my dying father is the bond I someday hope to achieve with my own patients. As a junior high school teacher, the warm and constructive relationships I established with my students and their parents were my greatest pride. I believe internal medicine is the specialty that offers me the best opportunity to develop such special, long-term relationships with patients. My personality will create an environment in which my patients will feel comfortable conveying not only medically vital information but also their psychosocial circumstances—critical to holistic care. Internal medicine also poses an exciting intellectual challenge to me: understanding the human body as a dynamic whole rather than as a collection of organs or processes. A love of the basic sciences was a main factor behind my initial attraction to medicine, and internal medicine both draws on and gives me an outlet for that love.

- I cannot say whether my ob-gyn career will involve a subspecialty like pelvic surgery, endocrinology, or urogynecology. However, I do know I will give obstetrics and gynecology equal emphasis. Dr. Goss told me that many ob-gyn physicians eventually stop practicing obstetrics because of the demanding schedule and on-call hours. But such "24/7" commitments do not intimidate me. I will not let anything constrain my ability to devote myself entirely to my patients. My philosophy of care will center on giving them more than they expect, which will include educating them in preventive care. At Grand Forks Community Hospital, I have discovered that many women unfortunately know very little about their reproductive health. One of my goals as a physician will be to help each patient understand her body so well that she won't think she needs to go the emergency room every time she has a yeast infection. For that reason, I would welcome an opportunity to serve in an underserved community.

- Although my training may some day involve a fellowship in a subspecialty of medicine, I intend to make a primary care practice my main focus. For me, a private practice supplemented by opportunities to teach would be my ideal career situation. Ten years from now, I will be done with my residency and establishing a practice of my own. As a primary care physician, I will donate my services to underserved communities by volunteering in clinics and by dividing my practice time equally between suburban clinical and urban hospital work. My practice will exemplify my philosophy of caregiving: Do more than is required to give the patient the best care possible, and treat patients the way I would like to be treated— with dignity and respect. I will strive to be not only a physician, but a confidant, counselor, and friend.

- As the postgenome era approaches, the basic knowledge I have acquired through years of research will help me translate both my clinical observations and my lab discoveries into newer methods of prevention and treatment for my patients. I look forward to being part of the "human face" of medicine and am confident that with the lessons of compassion I have learned from Drs. Bonham and Mogg, I can broaden my perspective in both the clinical and the basic science arenas.

- My personal goals center on writing academic articles and books on the philosophy of medicine and ethics, providing ethics consultation to medical professionals, and practicing internal medicine. I want to practice internal medicine because I believe medicine's fundamental philosophy should be grounded in the raw experience of medical practice and because my work in philosophy will help me address the larger existential and spiritual concerns of patients. Finally, gaining expertise in both clinical medicine and the philosophy of medicine will help me to be a lucid and credible ethics consultant and educator. With an MD/Ph.D. from Harvard I can pursue my personal goal of helping doctors and patients by shaping medicine's philosophical foundation for the century ahead.

- I look forward to a career in clinical pediatrics. In an age of managed care, pediatricians must focus on preventing disease and be willing to serve as patient advocates in the community. As such, I will work to help children and parents establish healthy habits, acknowledging the critical role played by environment and behavior in a child's progress toward a healthy adulthood. As a pediatrician I want to be a doctor, role model, and friend to my patients.

- While working as a public health educator in Darfur, I learned firsthand that infectious diseases have much higher incidence rates among those living in medically underserved areas. Hence, I intend to specialize in immunology and infectious diseases with a midsized medical group that has an academic affiliation so I can participate in clinical research.

Chapter 10 Perfect "Why Our School?" Phrases

"Why have you chosen to apply to Georgetown University School of Medicine, and how do you think your education at Georgetown will prepare you to become a physician for the future?"

(Georgetown University)

"Please briefly explain your interest in the Keck School of Medicine."

(USC)

Yes, it's true that you can get a sound medical education at any of the 129 schools accredited by the Association of American Medical Colleges. But do all these schools believe they're created equal? Of course not. Since your AMCAS essay is by necessity unspecific about which medical schools are your ultimate goal, many medical schools include secondary essay topics asking you to explain why you're applying to their programs in particular. As the following perfect phrases show, the best "Why our school?" statements go beyond the marketing verbiage found on schools' Web sites and focus on the applicant's personal knowledge of the program and its people.

■ I have chosen Oregon Health & Science University School of Medicine because it uses its rich teaching resources to benefit both its students and the larger community. Because OHSU lectures are taught by practicing physicians, students can gain firsthand exposure to the "end product" of the medical education—practicing physicians—while gaining real-world knowledge from them. I have personal experience with the quality of OHSU professors through my mentorship under Dr. Frederic Beecham, a cardiac surgeon at Doernbecher Children's Hospital and OHSU. Because he took the time to patiently explain the anatomy of the heart to me, I developed a strong interest in cardiology, which I hope to pursue at OHSU. OHSU's personal approach to teaching ensures that students are continually shown the practical importance of what they study—as well as how much more they still have to learn! Finally, I also admire the positive impact that OHSU has on the community. By emphasizing healing and community service—such as the required third-year rural community health clerkship and the Physician Assistant Program—OHSU trains students to value giving back to their community as public-minded future physicians.

■ Part of the oldest Catholic- and Jesuit-sponsored university in the United States, Georgetown University

School of Medicine shares my values. Its four-part longitudinal curriculum in clinical ethics and courses like "Religious Traditions of Health Care" and "The Role of Physician-Patient Relationships" instill a foundation of public service and principled integrity. This moral vision is also reflected in the liberating learning environment that Georgetown has created for its students. The pass/fail grading system will empower me to achieve in a less competitively stressful environment, and by reducing lecture-time requirements and giving me the freedom to choose my own electives, Georgetown allows me to take responsibility for shaping my own education. Georgetown's location in one of the most concentrated medical research hubs in the world is another compelling attraction for me. Situated within 10 miles of the National Institutes of Health and home to the Lombardi Cancer Center, Georgetown offers a cutting-edge five-year track for research-oriented students like me, in which I can spend an intensive 12 months between my second and third years pursuing my research interests. With a Georgetown education I will be well prepared to become a medical leader in the new century, no matter what it brings.

■ Born into this world weighing a mere two pounds, I was rushed to McMaster University Medical Center

(MUMC) where the pediatric staff fought round the clock to save my life. When my parents told me this story when I was a teenager, McMaster rose to the top of my short list for college applications. As a McMaster undergraduate I watched surgeries in MUMC's operating room, worked in its medical library, and as a student volunteer learned team skills watching MUMC's pathologists and residents share information in the GI rounds. Having learned, volunteered, and worked at McMaster, I know it well enough to unhesitatingly name DeGroote School of Medicine as my first choice for medical school. DeGroote is world renowned for its curriculum and excellence in obstetrics, pediatrics, and family medicine, and its department of clinical epidemiology and biostatistics is Canada's largest. Its innovations in problem-based learning, evidence-based health care, and small tutorial group learning demonstrate its commitment to practical, creative education and medicine. Shouldn't the institution that brought me into this world be the one that gives me the skills to maximize my impact in it?

- Northwestern University Feinberg School of Medicine offers me a truly comprehensive medical education. At Feinberg not only will I gain a strong basic science foundation, but I will also be able to explore nonscientific medical issues, from health-care system reform to the ethics of stem cell research, that empower future physicians to be effective in the ever-changing health-care system. Northwestern's Patient, Physician, and Society curriculum appeals to me because it focuses on interactions between patients and physicians as well as between physicians and society—the "one-on-one" and "one-to-many" relationships that interest me most. Because I have not decided on my medical specialty, Feinberg's multiple, uniformly outstanding facilities and expertise in all medical fields will give me the broadest opportunity to make an informed choice. Besides a well-rounded education, Feinberg's integrated, cross-disciplinary curriculum offers the ideal mix of traditional and problem-based learning. On the one hand, problem-solving skills ultimately determine the success of diagnosis and treatment, but before students can solve medical cases, they need the background information and guidance that focused lectures and discussion groups provide. Feinberg's curriculum integrates the best of both methods. Finally, through its Community Health, Devon, and Chinatown clinics, Feinberg will expose me to a great range of clinical experiences in one of the most diverse cities in the world. Through these free clinics Feinberg students who, like me, are interested in internal medicine can practice their clinical skills side by side with Northwestern physicians. I choose Feinberg because it is the complete medical school—offering rigor of instruction, wealth of resources, and values aligned with who I am.

■ As I researched Ohio State University College of Medicine, I learned about a school with a rich history of medical education innovation. But the more I learned, the more it was OSU's sheer diversity of resources that attracted me. With the Medical Center's fifteen clinical departments and six science departments, I can be assured of finding an area of medicine compatible with my ambitions. To help me define those ambitions, Ohio State offers two innovative curricular pathways to match my learning style and educational goals. I'm excited by the "block"-based body-systems focus of the integrated pathway because of its blend of lectures, case-based discussion, and clinical exposure. This interdisciplinary curriculum will enable me to become a truly well-rounded physician deeply grounded in analytical and managerial skills, medical humanities, and behavioral sciences and thus be ready to participate in all aspects of health care. Through OSU's Community Project I can begin gaining clinical exposure in my first year (the

OSU High Risk Perinatal Teen Program is especially attractive to me). Similarly, student assistantships will enable me to advance my education by participating in cutting-edge research opportunities at OSU, which *U.S. News* has ranked among the top 50 research schools. After comparing more than seven medical programs, I have concluded that my full potential as a physician can best be realized through the resources that Ohio State offers.

- Dr. James N. Thompson, MD, former dean of Wake Forest Medical School, once wrote that teaching medical schools must answer two crucial questions if they hope to address medicine's "moral imperatives" in our age of managed care and cost control: "what kind of person makes the best possible physician?" and "what constitutes the best possible training for that person?" I am applying to Wake Forest Medical School because I share Dr. Thompson's belief that these are medicine's central questions and because I believe that Wake Forest Medical School provides the most effective answer to them. What kind of person does make the best possible physician? Wake Forest's answer is its forward-thinking pedagogical philosophy, which inspired a redesigned curriculum built upon Dean Thompson's "ABCs" of aptitude, beneficence, and competence. By combining the best of the traditional and problem-based medical school curricula, Wake Forest integrates clinical exposure across the four-year learning experience—the perfect educational environment for students like me who are committed to becoming holistic caregivers. The innovation behind Wake Forest's new curriculum is a tradition at Wake Forest, the first medical school in the nation with a department of medical genetics, the institution where the first reimplantation of a severed human hand was performed, and the first medical school to completely adopt a problem-based learning curriculum. More importantly, given my interests, Wake Forest University Baptist Medical Center is one of only 1 percent of U.S. cancer centers that have been designated as comprehensive cancer centers by the National Cancer Institute. With such expertise and resources within arm's reach, you can rest assured that I will take advantage of Wake Forest's optional fourth-year Scholarly Project and will pursue a funded summer research opportunity in one of the medical school's cancer research projects. In short, at Wake Forest, I can be assured not only of acquiring a thorough, innovatively conceived foundation in medical knowledge, but of plenty of opportunities to conduct cutting-edge cancer research and gain clinical oncological exposure.

- I believe the Philadelphia College of Osteopathic Medicine offers me the best environment in which to pursue my goal of becoming a caring and compassionate osteopathic physician. PCOM is one of the best and largest osteopathic schools in the country, and has the distinction of being the civilian organization that produces the most physicians for the U.S. military. The PCOM students, like Lynn Christic and Erin Chang, I spoke with during my campus visit in April enthused about every aspect of the school, from the integrated curriculum and hands-on clinical exposure at PCOM's health-care centers to the flexibility in clerkship-related electives and the proactiveness of the Office of Student Affairs in supporting career placement. Everyone I talked to mentioned the optimal blend of classroom and clinical experience in PCOM's curriculum and the mixture of case methodologies and presentations, which injects a critical reality into the classroom. Last, given my research work on Alzheimer's at Gettysburg College, PCOM's interdisciplinary Center for Chronic Disorders of Aging is exciting for me, and I hope to participate in research at one of its collaborating institutions. For all these reasons, I know PCOM is the ideal school for me.

■ My specific interest in Uniformed Services University School of Medicine came into focus when I joined Radrix PharmaTherapies in 2006 as a protein biochemistry research associate developing heat-shock protein-based vaccines for cancer and chronic viral diseases. While learning molecular biology from Dr. Nathaniel McCain, I discovered that he had conducted research in the pathology lab of USU's Dr. Devin Ritterbusch. Dr. McCain energetically corrected my misconception that military medicine is only about combat casualty care and described USU Med School's impressive facilities and beautiful campus. He assured me that researchers weren't required to wear uniforms; in fact, many are civilians. The more I researched USU, the more I saw it as an institution comparable in every way to the leading health science centers, offering everything from a strong medical curriculum to world-class basic science research. For example, I discovered the depth of USU SOM's MD/Ph.D. program, which will enable me to build on the strengths I have gained at City of Hope Cancer Center and at Radrix. Speaking with USU second-year med student Alice Sierra, I learned about the great team-building and community opportunities available through Alpha Omega Alpha and the Courage to Care Health Campaign, and

Professor Anil Jain enthusiastically described the clinical and research experiences that await me at the Center for the Study of Traumatic Stress and the Center for Disaster and Humanitarian Assistance Medicine. And I would be dishonest if I denied the appeal of USU's tuitionless education and guaranteed four-year officer-grade salary!

■ I want to study medicine at the University of Washington because it is the best school in the United States for training family practice physicians (*U.S. News & World Report*). I have explored the "WWAMI" (Washington, Wyoming, Alaska, Montana, and Idaho) program firsthand at the university's Idaho and Pullman, Washington, campuses. Attending classes in anatomy, physiology, and neurology, I was impressed by Washington's capable, caring professors and the quality of its students. Because of the importance of research in my post-MD goals, Washington's sixth-place ranking nationally among research-oriented medical schools and its second-place status behind Harvard in NIH research funding are powerful draws for me. On a practical level, Washington's WWAMI program will give me a high-quality medical education without incurring tremendous debt, and this will allow me to focus immediately on my post-MD professional goal: serving underserved

➡

populations. Ideally, I will practice in a small rural town (10,000 or less) in Alaska or the Pacific Northwest while spending six weeks a year serving in underdeveloped countries. In this regard, the university's Rural/Urban Underserved Opportunities Program (R/UOP) WRITE program and International Health Group are big factors in my decision to choose Washington. Spending four weeks in a rural medical immersion experience after only my first year of medical school would be a really priceless educational opportunity.

■ When I first joined the USC Post Baccalaureate Pre-Med Program, I frankly didn't know what to expect. Going back to school with undergraduates, moving home with my parents, commuting to USC by train—it was a bit overwhelming at first. Today, I can say that my two years with the students, professors, and especially the advisors of USC have made all the difference in my medical school journey. In fact, my experience at USC is what prompted my interest in earning my MD at Keck. That interest solidified into a definite decision to apply when I learned about Keck's educational philosophy. Keck infuses the traditional with the practical by pioneering the introduction of clinical experiences during the first year. Working one on one with patients is why I chose medicine in the

➡

first place, so Keck's clinical emphasis will enable me to hit the ground running with a patient population—Los Angeles—that is one of the most diverse in the world. Keck's innovative curriculum, based on the thematic "standardized patient" model involving cases, small-group learning, and independent study, will give me the relevant education I will need to hone my skills as a compassionate health-care provider. And, since my interest is in clinical research involving biomedical technologies, I am also excited about Keck's expanding research in this area and the four new research facilities on the Health Sciences Campus, including the Zilkha Neurogenetic Institute. As one of the top 25 medical schools in the nation for federally sponsored research, Keck offers me extraordinary possibilities for developing my own research topics. Research strengths balanced with an emphasis on compassionate clinical care—Keck is the perfect fit for my interests and future plans.

- When I learned about Stanford's unique scholarly concentrations model I knew I had—to use a little consultantspeak—found my "power alley." Health Services and Policy Research will help me to define how technology can change health care by improving access to care and patient quality of life. Courses like "Rethinking International Health" and "Innovation and

Management in Health Care" are thrillingly relevant to the themes I helped Professor Dumas develop in his monograph, *A Future for Health Care*. When Dr. Ernesto Villon spoke about Stanford at the Sorbonne in 2006, I was impressed to learn about Stanford's amazing student-to-professor ratio and the freedom it gives students to define their focus. The optional fifth or sixth year will enable me to earn a joint degree (MPH), and Stanford's emphasis on independent research will let me explore my interest in technology and health care and learn from thought-leading faculty advisors like Dr. Alain Enthoven, the "father of managed competition." Stanford balances all these strengths with early exposure to clinical care and to patients— both my starting point and ultimate purpose in choosing a medical career.

■ The oldest medical school in New Jersey, New Jersey Medical School is my first choice for medical school. First, NJMS's Jubilee Curriculum, integrating basic sciences and clinical experiences, captures exactly the way I want to learn medicine—holistically. To gain the clinical experience I crave, NJMS's Physician Core course will let me get started in the first semester of my first year. NJMS's teaching hospital, The University Hospital, and its Level I Trauma Center—New Jersey's busiest—offer me exposure to the wide variety of patients I'll be serving throughout my career. Because I'm moving from a career in graphic design and advertising back to my science roots, I've enjoyed learning how to conduct research over the past 18 months at Rutgers. NJMS's stem cell initiatives and opportunities in counterterrorism and biodefense-related research are very exciting for me. To join NJMS and become part of its rich history and tradition of excellence is an opportunity I would cherish.

■ The University of Chicago Pritzker School of Medicine is an ideal fit for me on many levels, but particularly in its small and diverse student body, extraordinarily close relationship with the larger university, and emphasis on treating human disease through an integrated approach to discovery and patient care. By focusing on the relevance of basic sciences to clinical medicine and by emphasizing problem solving, small groups, and patient contact, Pritzker's curriculum appeals directly to my strengths. Biomedical research is my passion, so Pritzker's tradition of cutting-edge research, Medical Education Research Grants, and its wealth of conferences will enable me to translate that knowledge to the bedside. Similarly, because knowledge of human physiology and disease is continually expanding, the school's new Pritzker Curriculum Initiative, location within the university's biological sciences division, and full-time teaching faculty assure me of interdisciplinary exposure to the latest developments in science and medicine. Not least, I'm eager to attend a medical school in Chicago, whose richly diverse inner-city population will expose me to the most urgent medical challenges.

Part III

Perfect Phrases for Personal Topics

Chapter 11 Perfect Autobiographical Phrases

"If you could present yourself to the Committee on Admissions, what would you want to make sure they knew about you?"

(Michigan State University)

"What is one life experience you want to talk about?"

(Albany Medical College)

"Who would you consider to be the most influential person in your life and why?"

(UC Davis)

M ost AMCAS essays focus on the applicant's decision to become a doctor, leaving the admissions committee in the dark about personal experiences that might make the applicant an appealing addition to the medical school's class. That's why many schools pose secondary essay topics to learn about their applicants' personal stories: to meet the person behind the MCAT score, grades, and clinical and research experiences. As we'll see in this chapter's perfect phrases, stories about your family background and upbringing, key moments in your life, or important people or influences in your development can give medical schools the personal insights they seek.

Childhood, Family, and Upbringing

■ After three years of hard work at my Kansas boarding school, far from home, I finally received my diploma. When I stepped off the plane at Singapore's Changi Airport, I eagerly searched for my parents in the crowd. Instead, I saw my uncles, each with a gloomy look on his face. "Your dad had a heart attack last week while playing tennis," Uncle Ji said, his voice trembling, "and they couldn't save him." I froze, stunned. Tears flooded my eyes as I pictured my father's lopsided smile and heard his gravelly voice. Not only had I lost a loving and caring father but also a role model who supported the family. In the days that followed, my mother, who my younger brother, Kaiwen, and I once turned confidently to for help, became physically and emotionally fragile. Kaiwen, stunned by the unexpected loss, became depressed and helpless. It was suddenly up to me to remain strong so the family could function. I began making all my family's decisions, from organizing the funeral to planning for our financial future. My father's premature death—easily the worst moment of my life—accelerated my maturation, helped me become independent, and forced me for the first time to deal with death.

- I was born with developmental dysplasia of the hip. If my condition had not been corrected, I would have limped for the rest of my life. When I did not respond to the manual reduction treatment method, I was operated on at Deaconess Children's Hospital of Eureka Springs, Arkansas. Fortunately, the operation was a success, and after a few years of rehabilitation I could look forward to a normal life. Two memories from my experiences at Deaconess will always stand out. The first was the relationship of trust I formed with my orthopedic surgeon, Dr. Barry Matsugawa. Every hour, he would come in to check on me, always treating me like a member of his own family. The special, very personal attention Dr. Matsugawa gave me lifted me out of my fear and anxiety. My second memory from Deaconess is that most of the other children faced even bigger challenges than I did. These children, ranging everywhere from seven to fourteen years old, were permanently disabled and in constant pain, yet to my amazement they always kept their spirits up and did everything they were asked to do to the best of their abilities. From their courage,

I learned to never give up. Seeing these children befriend each other and rally to each other's aid helped me to understand the concept of teamwork in new ways. Disabled, I have learned, does not mean "unabled"—these kids' ability to work together as a team was as natural and sincere as any "normal" group of people I've met. I also felt a deep desire to help these children and children like them and knew from that point forward what I wanted to be when I grew up. My philosophy of the medical profession is based on this early and extended experience with medicine from the patient's perspective: I will be able to offer my future patients genuine empathy because I know the pain and fear they are experiencing.

■ Growing up in an isolated valley of the Ch'ang-pai Mountains, I had a burning desire—unsatisfied until I was eight—to see what was on the other side of the summits surrounding our home. My father, a tax collector, was the first in his family to attend college, and he raised me to understand the value of education and self-reliance. In 1998, my family and I immigrated to the United States, but when my grandfather fell terminally ill a year later, my parents returned to China to care for him. I was only 17, but I made a gut decision to stay in the United States and fend for myself, against my parents' direct wishes. As a child of a culture in which obeying one's elders is bred in the bone, it took everything I had to disobey my parents. I was on my own.

■ Every Sunday, my sisters and I would find ourselves engrossed in our grandmother's stories about how naughty my father was as a kid, the hardships of the Vietnamese War, or what our grandfather Thieu was like. So when grandma suddenly started forgetting parts of her stories, we noticed immediately. I remember the helpless looks we all gave each other when my father told us that she had been diagnosed with Alzheimer's. There was no drug to give, no organ to transplant, no surgery to perform. Month by month, then week by week, some unknown force within my grandmother's brain robbed her of the qualities that made my grandmother "mine." When I questioned her doctors, they tried to be informative, but their answers finally came down to a frustrated, "We don't really know." Alzheimer's and the inability of my grandmother's doctors to help her first made me realize that the intellectual curiosity that fueled my love of science could only truly justify itself if it improved people's lives. My grandmother's memory has always enabled me to resist doing research for its own sake, to always ask, "Who can this benefit?" She is the primary reason I want to pursue a career in academic medicine.

➡

- My family dreaded Monday, Wednesday, and Friday nights. On those days, nervous anticipation made the dinner table quiet and the food difficult to eat. Everyone was wondering, "Should we get it over with or put it off as long as we can?" Once we decided to go ahead, my father summoned my sister Samantha and cleaned her quadriceps with alcohol. "One more minute, just one more minute, please!" Samantha pleaded. My father always patiently waited until my sister was ready. "Relax your leg, Sammie. It'll hurt less," he gently advised. After Samantha's final deep breath and terrified go-ahead nod, my father plunged the needle into the tense leg muscle at a perfect ninety-degree angle. My mother and I could only hold our breaths and pray the pain would not be as bad as the time before. It was only last year that my father admitted to me how difficult it was to have to administer my sister's intramuscular growth hormone injections over the nine long years of "shot nights."

- I have a very special brother. Curtis was born with a rare genetic disorder called methylmalonic acidemia and homocystinuria (MA&H) that affects one in 50,000 fetuses. Diagnosed late, he suffers from hydrocephalus and major developmental disabilities like cortical blindness, small brain matter, and delayed development. Since MA&H is now curable in early stages, Curtis is one of the oldest living patients. His impact on my life has been enormous. I first became interested in science to better understand what had happened to him, and eventually I majored in nutrition, which taught me the chemistry behind Curtis's disorder. Watching him doggedly survive all his problems taught me to be a fighter in my own right. After my first semester at Haverford, for example, I seriously doubted I could handle the intense academics. Inspired by Curtis, however, I sought help and persevered; my grades improved every semester. But perhaps the greatest thing Curtis taught me is to extend my compassion beyond the confines of our family by dedicating myself to help others. Curtis's disorder gave me firsthand exposure to the critical role that pediatricians play in the quality of life for both the patient and the patient's family. He has been a driving force in my decision to become a pediatrician.

Key Experiences

- During my junior year in high school my father received a different kind of emergency call. One fall day my Aunt Suzie, whose family lived on our street, ran up to our house breathless and panicked, crying out to my father to come help. My father grabbed a cell phone, and we sprinted to her back barn. There we found my Uncle Drew lying unconscious with a gaping head laceration and the potent smell of car exhaust hanging in the air. As he worked on his car with the engine running, the barn door had closed without him noticing, and when he succumbed to the carbon monoxide, he had struck his head on a shovel. As my father started cardiopulmonary resuscitation, I immediately called 911. After requesting help, I began helping my father with CPR, but the look in his eyes told me to stop. We had come too late. My uncle was dead.

- The year was 2003. I sat in Dr. Krull's hard metal office chair waiting for the test results that would change my life. When Dr. Krull walked in, he immediately sat down opposite me with a sober expression that scared me out of my wits. "Nellie, your enlarged lymph nodes can have two causes. They may be simply the result of a virus, the most likely case. But it is also possible they are a form of cancer." My eyes began to tear up as he continued. "The only way we can tell whether the lymph nodes are malignant is to perform a biopsy, and, of course, we need to do this as soon as possible. I have it scheduled for Thursday. Is that okay for you?" I could not believe this was really happening. I was 17 years old—in the prime of my teenage

years—and I was being told I could have a life-
threatening disease. Unable to respond, unable to
move, I could only watch his mouth explain that my
lymph nodes' rapid pace of growth "was consistent
with" cancer. I do not remember anything he said
after that. As my mother prepared me for Thursday
afternoon, I slipped into a state of numbed disbelief.

■ I can still recall that hot, humid July day in the Florida
Panhandle and the feeling I had as I drove up to my
grandmother's house only to see an ambulance sitting
in the driveway. Running into the house, I discovered
that the paramedics were preparing to transport my
grandmother to the hospital. I suddenly felt overcome
by powerlessness. For years, my grandmother had
battled breast cancer and survived, but on this July
day the disease had caught up with her, and she
would never awaken from the coma it had induced in
her. The only thing that redeemed the awful day was
the compassion her physicians showed her and my
family at the hospital as we prepared to say goodbye
to her. One of the physicians even asked us to gather
around grandmother's bed as he said a prayer for her,
my grandfather, and the rest of our family.

■ The impact of moving to Manhattan from Djakarta for
college was both subtle and total. Although my values
are the same, I now have a much deeper confidence in

➡

my instincts. I know I can adapt to new challenges and learn unfamiliar topics quickly. And though living overseas has given me a greater appreciation for being American, I now see myself as a "permanent" citizen of the most mysterious and exciting city in the world.

- It was only 10 days into basic training when our drill sergeant told us to retrieve our enlistment contracts from our wall lockers. Sitting mute on the polished tiles, we all read for the first time the clause that says you can be reassigned "in time of war." Sergeant Alvarez then turned on the television, and we grimly watched scenes of warfare in Afghanistan. We had been reassigned to infantry training—next stop: Operation Enduring Freedom. Surviving boot camp at Camp Lejeune became my rite of passage, a journey into the deepest part of me. Over the next several weeks, I overcame my fears and doubts and learned how to guide a squad of men shaken by suicides and an unforeseen war into becoming more than they had known how to be before. I began my nineteenth year as a boy surrounded by strangers. I emerged from it leading men who had become my brothers.

- Saltine crackers—it is hard to imagine that these dry, tasteless biscuits were at the top of my older brother's wish list the summer he turned eight. That July Irfan had suffered a brain aneurysm that required two surgeries and an extended hospital stay. Because of his post-surgical nausea and resulting inability to hold down any solid food, these bland crackers were the only food Irfan craved. When the nurse informed him that the hospital cafeteria had no saltines, the composure Irfan had maintained so bravely for three weeks fell apart, and his pain and frustration at being ill boiled to the surface. As we helplessly watched the tears stream down Irfan's face, Dr. Boniface quietly stepped out of the room only to return a short while later with a box of saltines behind his back. Sitting with Dr. Boniface, contentedly munching crackers and discussing baseball, Irfan briefly escaped the horrors of dizziness, bedpans, the permanent scar on the back of his head, and, worst, the fear of never being the same again—of never being able to hit a baseball again, play the piano, or even walk properly. Dr. Boniface's treatment of Irfan went past "medical attention" and became something much bigger: it accelerated Irfan's recovery by allowing him to be a normal eight-year-old once more when the world he had known suddenly crumbled around him. This doctor's gesture had a huge impact on my six-year-old's vision of the world and marked the beginning of my interest in medicine.

➡

■ I almost didn't recognize him. When I saw my grandfather for the last time in the summer of 2003, he had been unconscious for days. Half his face was covered by an oxygen mask, and his body seemed tiny amidst the beeping machines in his Seoul hospital room. How was it possible that this brave man who as a student activist and politician had helped bring democracy to South Korea had become so frail and small? My grandfather had been diagnosed with lung cancer in 1997, and since then everyone in the family had taken turns going back to Seoul to spend time with him. Seeing the man I admired so much fight courageously but futilely with death, I felt frustration at my inability to help. Grandpa's brave battle with death ended later that summer, but it left me with an intense desire to acquire the medical knowledge to save the lives of people like him who suffer through the pain of wasting illness.

Role Models

■ The physicians' axiom, "First do no harm," has special meaning for my father because it's not merely part of his creed as a doctor but is deeply rooted in his Hindu values. Born and raised in rural Gujarat, he earned a scholarship to UCLA at the age of 16. Confronted with the stark cultural contrasts between his new land and his old, it was his ideals—stemming largely from his Hindu upbringing—that gave him the integrity to endure. I inherited his untiring endurance and was taught to embrace his belief that life should be lived honestly and evaluated in moral terms. Ironically, it was because of my father's overwhelming commitment to medicine that I was initially not attracted to the profession. Even today, I can vividly remember my trips to the ER dormitory—the only way I could see my busy father. I eventually realized that he was willing to make such sacrifices because of the pure satisfaction helping people gave him. I believe that satisfaction is intimately related to the integrity and unrelenting care that he brings to the practice of medicine.

■ Not until we saw Dr. Rubbra at New York University did I understand what it really means to be a great physician. Dr. Rubbra spent many hours of his time with Kimber and my parents just listening, consoling, and caring. After the first visit, he told her, "What you have is real. I don't know what it is, but I am going to work as hard as I can until I find out." Kimber burst into tears. Just to hear that someone believed her, in spite of what the tests said, and would stay committed to her despite frustrating results was the greatest thing my sister could have heard. For the first time someone understood that regardless of how her illness appeared from the outside, it was life-changing for her. Dr. Rubbra had placed Kimber into occupational therapy to help her relearn how to live her life. Though exhaustion had left her isolated and lonely, therapy taught her how to conserve enough energy to spend time with friends, if only once a week. Because of Dr. Rubbra's empathy, he could truly hear that what Kimber needed before a diagnosis was some semblance of a normal life. Kimber's condition was recently diagnosed as postviral encephalitis, but there is still no long-term prognosis. My original image of a physician was not too different from that of a mechanic: a technician who fixes a problem. But Dr. Rubbra's treatment of my sister made me realize that the ability to not only treat an illness but to help a patient cope with the changed reality of his or her life is the mark of a truly great physician.

■ "Hello, friend." This simple phrase was my introduction to medicine. They were the words that greeted me every time I visited my pediatrician, Dr. Ward Mangan. Young children do not like to be caged up in a room with a complete stranger who looks up their nose, peeps in their ears, and inspects their toes with callused, adult hands. But without fail, Dr. Mangan's friendly smile always calmed my fears and made the four sterile white walls disappear from view. During one "emergency" visit to his office, I saw a grin bloom on my father's face as Dr. Mangan explained that the abnormal bump on my left wrist was nothing more than a cyst filled with water—not the malignant growth my mother had feared. It was this combination of skills I discovered in Dr. Mangan—healing through kindness and through teaching—that 15 years later still explains why I am so strongly drawn to a career in medicine.

"Let's go see Mrs. Jenns," was Dr. Brian Melman's way of recruiting me for an after-hours shadowing session late last year. It was 9 p.m., and he had already been on call for two days—he couldn't have slept more than a few hours, and he looked it. Yet, though 30 years my senior, he looked ready to climb Mt. Everest—or pay a house call to a dying patient. Dr. Melman inspires me with his intelligence and clinical expertise but also with his indefatigable attitude. For him, pharmacology, physiology, biochemistry, all the scientific aspects of medicine, are just gateways to the more rewarding subject: helping sick people. Already contemplating med school, I asked him how he maintains his energy and enthusiasm. "It's easy. As bad as I sometimes feel, and sometimes that's pretty rotten, I know that what the patient is going through is much worse."

- My brother Jason was my friend, my first mentor, and my toughest competitor. When he became our state's high school wrestling champion in 2000, I practiced with and learned from him until in 2001 I took the title from him. When he handed me the tournament cup at the awards ceremony, he gave me his "Keep tryin', little brother—it won't help" smile and whispered in my ear: "You'll be giving this back to me next year."
I excelled in sports, school, and life because of the determination and leadership I learned from Jason. Telling me, "I want to serve my country," he became a Special Forces volunteer in Iraq in 2003. Although a sniper's bullet took him from me 18 months ago, he'll always be the person I look up to the most.

- Even today, the people of Brockton, Ohio, still debate how my grandfather survived. Five years ago, while he was crossing the street in the farming town he rarely left, my 78-year-old grandfather was struck by a speeding car and lay in the deserted road for almost an hour before a neighbor found him. He lost his leg in the accident, but amazingly he never voiced any anger or desire for vengeance. "The driver probably didn't see me" he charitably offers and regrets only that running his farm is harder now. When relatives advised my grandfather to sell his farm and move to Columbus where we could look after him, he protested that that would be like losing his other leg, and he never let us raise the subject again. After the operation he bought farm equipment that he could operate with one leg and continued running his organic farm with the same tirelessness as before. Everything takes him longer now, but even at 83 his farm is productive, and he remains the simple, cheerful man he always was. I thought a lot about my grandfather as I contemplated abandoning a career in my father's dairy business for medical school. He was the only member of my family to encourage my career switch, though he could easily have chosen to view it as a rejection of the vocation he's devoted his life to.

Chapter 12 Perfect Phrases for Challenges and Disadvantage

"Describe your toughest challenge in life thus far and how you handled it."

(Wayne State University)

"If you feel that you have encountered significant disadvantages and would like the Admissions Committee to take them into consideration, you are invited (not required) to provide this additional information."

(University of Wisconsin)

M edical schools believe they can find out a lot about how applicants will deal with the challenges of medical school by seeing how they've dealt with the challenges they've encountered in life. Applicants who can show they've come through a lot to get where they are today will be viewed with special favor by admissions readers happy to reward determination and focus. Making difficult decisions, overcoming obstacles, battling through resistance—all of these can be powerful material for essays about challenge. Let's look at some challenge and disadvantage perfect phrases.

157

- I was a sophomore in high school when my father decided to take a job in Texas. My brother and I were to stay in Florida with our mother to finish our schooling and then join him in San Antonio in the new house he planned to buy there. He did buy that house, moving all our furniture there, while we continued to live in a small furnished one-bedroom near the projects. But the original one-year separation expanded into two years and then two and a half. When my father finally told us we could pack up for Texas, I was beginning college in Tallahassee and decided against transferring. Incensed, my father informed me that I could pay for my college education on my own—beginning with next quarter's tuition check! Two years later, I was making slow progress toward my degree while balancing a 35-hour workweek, when my mother called to say my father had "fallen in love" and wanted a divorce. My mother's tone of voice, one I'd never heard before, told me it was time for me to fly to Texas and help her and my brother cope. College would have to wait.

- While I was looking for an NGO to help me, I found myself in Bujumbura in front of a sign that read, "Burundi National Progress Trust." In a thick French accent, Dr. Domitian Ndadaye, a retired doctor who came to manage the site once a month, described the

➡

"rehabilitation" protocol: "We keep them here for three days, and by that time they are cured." Swallowing my urge to question this "regimen," I resolved to create change from within and began building trust with my two fellow volunteers, both struggling former bhang addicts. I was convinced that a 12-step program could succeed in Burundi and set about developing and implementing a model adapted to the local idiom. I spent many late nights next to a lantern with a third-grade Kirundi grammar book, an English-Kirundi dictionary, chalk, and the wooden crates I used to fashion signs for each of the 12 steps, which I then nailed to the wall of our meeting place. The other volunteers laughed at my crude attempts at first, but they helped nonetheless. Within a few weeks I felt more confident in the language and ready to facilitate classes and discussions with actual patients. As attendance in these classes grew, gradually I gained the trust of Dr. Ndadaye and convinced him to invest in a library and gym for the patients. After a year, I have developed close relationships with some patients. I have visited their villages, met and spoken with their families, and even become their friends.

■ It looked like it was going to get ugly. My first week at Henderson County Youth Shelter, a short-term alternative youth program for male adolescents in

Las Vegas, I shadowed another counselor to understand the many tasks we all do at the home: cooking meals, performing the chores, making sure the kids have clothes to wear, and so on. In only my second week there I was getting the teenagers ready for bed—hygiene and music until 9:30 and then lights out—when Hector, a 16-year-old with a history of crime, began to get rowdy. Calling on his peers to "blow this place," he began jumping around from peer to peer trying to get them to follow his lead. I was alone, and the night shift did not begin till 11:30. As the younger teenagers began to respond to Hector's incitement, I tried to assure them, with limited success, that it was not in their best interests to walk out of this open-door program. Realizing that I had only minutes to deescalate the situation, I had to act decisively. I could call juvenile detention to remove Hector, but that might lead to a struggle and Hector's reassignment to jail. I decided to tackle the problem directly: I demanded that he go back to bed. Hector laughed off my command by saying he didn't have to listen to any "country boy" from Maine who didn't know what it was like growing up on the streets of North Vegas. Realizing I needed to make a connection with him, I began to converse with him in Spanish, asking him to sit with me at the desk "just to talk."

I made no threats or ultimatums; I gave Hector my full attention and asked him what was going on ("¿Que pasa?"). Twenty minutes later, I had learned about his tough childhood as a single-parent child and early brushes with gangs and alcoholism. Hector's long life narrative—and perhaps his surprise at my interest—diffused his anger. I turned the shelter's lights out that night with no "insurrection" or escaped inmates. My conversations with Hector continued nightly for the next two weeks. When he told me he didn't want to return to a life of crime in North Las Vegas, I saw my opening and invited him to help me run some shelter activities. His response over the next month was incredible. He became active both in his treatment and in house events, and he developed into a true leader. After graduating from the program a year later, he regularly came back to say hello and let us know he was doing fine.

■ My father was born in the wilds of northern Wyoming but after earning a scholarship to Yale and then a JD at Harvard Law, he settled in Manhattan, where he met and eventually married my mother. After I finished fourth grade, my parents decided to spend a year in Paris and sent me to live with my grandparents in the small Wyoming ranching town of Rail Gap. Even at my resilient young age the lifestyle contrasts between Rail

Gap and the Upper East Side were a major shock. Instead of the personal maid who had prepared my choice of breakfasts on East 89th Street, I had to quickly develop culinary self-sufficiency when my grandparents told me the only "vittles" were biscuits and cream gravy. Instead of a five-minute limousine ride to The Brearley School, I found myself thrown into the Wyoming winter cold every morning for a bumpy 45-minute bus ride to Rail Gap Elementary, a place that perfectly conformed to my mental image of a penitentiary for the criminally insane.

- Shanice, a 17-year-old high school senior, was a patient on our floor when she suffered, through no identifiable human error, an extremely rare brain injury during a routine appendectomy. This unusual complication—its etiology remains unexplained—left her completely paralyzed. Her hearing, vision, and sense of touch were fine, but she could not blink, talk, walk, or move any other muscle voluntarily. Every day, virtually everyone in her high school came to Roosevelt Memorial's ICU to see Shanice. I too saw her daily, even held her hand and spoke to her and her friends and family. It was heartrending beyond words to see her lying still in her bed when shortly before she had been laughing and joking with the nurses and her baby brother, Trevon. During Shanice's stay in the ICU, I came home every night emotionally exhausted and angry that such an inexplicable calamity could have occurred to so healthy and vivacious a girl. After six weeks Shanice developed pneumonia and died. I tried to seek solace in older colleagues' assurances that eventually you learn to compartmentalize your emotions over patients whose personalities, hopes, and pains are so vividly on display, but they didn't help. Was I really cut out for a medical career?

■ During my last three years at Occidental College I worked long hours as both a phlebotomist and then as an EKG technician. After my first days of training and blood-drawing practice on fellow workers and healthy patients, I was sent off to do my first solo blood draw in the ER. I was handed one of the toughest cases: an elderly woman with multiple chronic illnesses and an arm whose "good" veins had all been stuck repeatedly. To add to the pressure, anxious family members crowded into the tiny prison-block-sized room, suspiciously following my every move. After missing her vein twice, I was close to giving up and seeking help, but decided to try once more. Using a tiny "butterfly" needle, I found the vein! In my haste to finish, however, I inflicted on myself the phlebotomist's worst nightmare—a needle stick. Racing back to the lab, I soaked my finger in Betadine,

➡

and felt my heart sink as I learned that I would have to undergo six months of testing. Luckily, the woman was fine and had no serious infections.

- Hearing is something young people take for granted, and I was no different. In my quest to be a professional drummer and singer, developing a hearing condition was the furthest thing from my mind. Unfortunately, in practicing and performing for a musical career, I was exposed to noise louder than the human auditory system was meant to take, and I developed hyperacusis—a painful sensitivity to normal environmental sounds. In addition to persistent tinnitus, I experienced physical pain when doors were shut and phones rang around me, and even running water and normal conversation could cause me discomfort. When I heard certain high-pitched sounds, I would feel dizzy and nauseous. Normal careers, let alone a musical one, seemed impossible.

- "I don't want to do this." I could practically hear myself thinking the words as the reality of Al's absence hit home. Suddenly, the hospital hall that had been busy with people felt lonely and cold. Just 20 hours before I had been standing in this same hallway on my first volunteer assignment at Stamford Hospital, having my first conversation with Al, an elderly patient who had bowel removal surgery a few days before. He seemed distressed, so I went over to him and asked if he needed anything. "No dear," he said, "I'm just getting some exercise." That was the beginning of a friendly exchange after which I walked him back to his bed and told him I'd see him tomorrow. On my way home that evening, I reflected fondly on the satisfactions of patient interaction I'd experienced on my first day as a volunteer. The following day I went to greet Al, and to my surprise saw a new patient in his bed. The nurse informed me that Al had suffered cardiac arrest the night before and had "expired." "You mean he died?" I asked stupidly. I didn't want to believe what I was hearing. Traumatized and depressed by the news, I signed out for the day. Over the next few days, I began to question my career goals. If I couldn't cope with the loss of a patient, then maybe I wasn't cut out for medicine.

- In the spring of 1999, my younger sister QiaoQiao was diagnosed with a rare case of skin cancer and given three to six months to live. I believed—I knew—she would survive. In the meantime, she was spending her time in the hospital, missing school and morbidly preoccupied with her illness. I decided to tutor her in math and English. Soon, some of my friends started volunteering to help entertain QiaoQiao too. Gathering informally a few times a week, we quickly befriended

➡

other kids in the ward and began entertaining them with books, videogames, and comics.

■ That inspiring success story was dealt a serious blow when I developed anorexia at age 14. After struggling for two years against this debilitating eating disorder, I was admitted to a hospital program the summer before my sophomore year. At St. Luke's, I met girls like myself who were so malnourished they had to limit how much they walked to minimize the calories they burned. Other girls hadn't successfully kept a meal down for many months. The St. Luke's program taught us how to gain weight and meet our nutritional needs, but it also gave me my first lesson in how inadequately the American health-care system treats mental illness. I won't forget my anger when I first learned that girls I had grown to care about were forced to leave our $1,250-a-day program despite dangerously low blood pressure, osteoporosis, or irregular heartbeat—all because their inpatient treatment insurance coverage was limited or had expired.

■ When my father moved our family from Egypt to the United States in 1990, he sacrificed a solid career, a comfortable lifestyle, and a respected role in Cairo's academic community so that my sister and I could receive American educations. Despite his Ph.D. and extensive curriculum vitae, he struggled in America,

➡

working as an assistant professor at a community college for five years before trying to strike out on his own as a consulting engineer—with mixed results. When I asked him once why he had made all these sacrifices, he said only that we were not only his children but his duty. I lost my chance to fully thank him for this gift when he unexpectedly died of a heart attack in 1997, a week before his forty-seventh birthday. My father's legacy of integrity, determination, and selflessness kept me going as I, though only 12, tried to be the "man in the family" for my devastated mother.

- "Oh my God, you were placed at Cherry Street!" My teacher-in-training classmates at Concordia University consoled me as word spread that my first trial-by-fire as a public school teacher would occur in one of the Twin Cities' least "comfortable and convenient" schools—Cherry Street High School in St. Paul's tough inner city. Soon, I learned some of the grim details about Cherry Street: a school administrator had been gunned down when his shady business dealings went awry, a child of one of the teachers assaulted someone with a deadly weapon, and so on. I can't say I was surprised then when on my first day in class my students challenged me directly, complaining, "Why do we have to learn this?" Seeing that at Cherry Street respect had to be earned, I began telling them my story. As a high school student, I had hated studying and much preferred the basketball court, until a teacher who knew my family informed me that if I scored well enough on the SAT, I could earn scholarships to college—enabling my mother to quit one of the two jobs she was working to fund my education. By overcoming my fear of mathematics, I earned a high enough score to win a tuition-free ride at the University of Wisconsin. When my Cherry Street students realized that my background was no different from theirs, they began to see me as a role model for their own success. I did have to send the occasional student to detention, but most gradually showed motivation to learn. Two months later, when I stayed late to help the students prepare for the SAT, the entire class showed up.

■ My wife Dawn had had morning sickness before, but this was something different. Early into her pregnancy, Dawn's symptoms worsened, so I had her move back to Atlanta where her parents could take better care of her and our two-year-old daughter, Aimee. When Dawn began repeatedly vomiting blood, however, I took an advance leave and immediately returned to Georgia. The test results showed high levels of thyroid hormones—harmless if caused by pregnancy, but, if they were preexisting, they could potentially affect both Dawn and our baby. I immediately requested a leave of absence from my analyst's position and stayed by Dawn's hospital bed until she and the baby were fine. I was shocked to learn on my return three weeks later that all my work had been reassigned to another analyst. The manager I had willingly sacrificed evenings and weekends for for two years muttered something about "needing people we can count on" and indicated vaguely that the promotion he had promised had "encountered some resistance." Two months later I was downsized. Though I was devastated, Dawn's illness had reminded me of what I really care about. We are resolved to love and care for our new child, normal or not, and our lives will probably never be the same. I know now that I will succeed in transitioning into medicine, but I also know what I didn't before: that my most important consideration now will always be the needs and wishes of my family. They will always come first.

Chapter 13 Perfect Diversity Phrases

"The recruitment of a diverse student body is a major goal of the University of Pittsburgh's Medical School Admissions Committee. Please tell us whether facets of your life, background or education to date would contribute to the achievement of this goal."

(University of Pittsburgh)

Medical schools want diverse classes—period. Indeed, diversity is such a critical concern that many schools invite applicants to submit a secondary essay exclusively on that topic. Fortunately, they define "diversity" quite loosely. Aside from race and gender, your personal or family history, your religion and cultural background, your international and travel experiences, and your hobbies and passions are all fair game as diversity essay topics. Let's look at some diversity perfect phrases.

■ Sometimes the best way to understand the society you belong to is to leave it. Moving with my parents to Warsaw when I was seven gave me an early and intense curiosity about cultural dissimilarities that I still possess after living in five cities on four continents. Why do Norwegians toast so formally? Why do Turks waste so much water? Why are chopsticks plastic in Chinese restaurants, metal in Korea, and wood everywhere else? The 16 years I've spent living, traveling, and working outside the United States have helped me answer some of these questions, and in doing so understand myself and America better. Because I ultimately define myself as American, I am returning to the United States to earn my medical degree. But I'll never forget that it's the perspective I've gained from living in Brazil, Sudan, Korea, and Germany that gives me the confidence to make that decision.

■ As the truck, lurching and groaning, lowered the yellow monster to the ground, I thought to myself, "What have I gotten myself into this time?" I had rented the massive thing with only a phone call and a credit card number, so how hard could this be, right? Upon witnessing my awe at the Cat's size, the deliveryman decided that I, a 23-year-old female, probably needed a quick operational lesson. His lecture all too quickly completed, the kind deliveryman gave me a wink and

➡

a nod and left me sitting atop a shiny yellow Caterpillar backhoe loader. Leveling the playing surface of a softball field and then building a 10-foot warning track are hardly tasks to be taken lightly, let alone by a driver uninitiated in the mysteries of manual transmission. But they were unquestionably mine, because as the assistant softball coach at Dakota Regents University, my duties included "ballfield maintenance," as well as recruiting, tutoring, coordinating planned giving, road-trip arranging, film analysis, and bookkeeping. After numerous attempts, I finally figured out how to drive a stick-shift; how to navigate all the levers, buttons, and switches to do what I wanted to do; and how to scrape and level while in reverse (don't ask)—all with only minimal damage to the school's facility. The fact that I possess the skills to operate a bulldozer is, I admit, not grounds for admitting me as a diversity candidate, but I believe the reasons behind my bulldozing ability surely are. Let me explain.

■ My Japanese upbringing has played a large role in my life. In my early years, I lived on USC's campus while my mother attended graduate school. As a result, my neighbors and classmates were the children of graduate students from all over the world. My baseball, soccer, and tennis teammates had names like Shinsako, Buchan, Tjarko, Yze Tsu, Rava, Vladimir, and Kareem.

My experiences playing, studying, and competing with them made me more understanding and comfortable with all types of people in any situation. While encouraging my exposure to a diverse community, my parents and grandparents also taught me to embrace my Japanese heritage. I accompanied them to Buddhist temple every week and dressed in a kimono to celebrate our ancestors during Obon festival. In high school, I studied Japanese, and at USC, I cherished the opportunity to spend six months studying overseas in Japan. Thus, in addition to my education and biomedical research background, I believe my cultural background will enable me to contribute to the school's diversity.

■ The proud product of my family's public service heritage, I'm excited about contributing my knowledge and abilities to benefit my patients and the medical profession. My multicultural experiences in Portugal and in Chicago's inner-city communities have given me the confidence and knowledge to communicate with a culturally diverse population. As a student at DePaul University, I have demonstrated an unusual commitment to thoroughly exploring a medical career. I didn't just accumulate lab experience; I won grants and a Howard Hughes internship. I didn't just rack up clinical emergency room experience;

I rode an ambulance as an EMT trainee into Chicago's toughest neighborhoods. Finally, I didn't just get my ticket punched at American Medical Student Association lectures; I became co-chair of Chicago MED. I have always tried to bring a little extra to my "premed" activities. Doing so has helped me develop my initiative and leadership skills while teaching me how to work efficiently in a team. I am confident that I can bring the heritage, enthusiasm, and abilities I brought to DePaul to my Tulane classmates as well.

- The beauty and complexity of salsa was unlike anything I had ever experienced. After completing my Introduction to Dance class, I built on my rudimentary knowledge of salsa by taking lessons twice a week at a local dance school. The first three months of lessons were excruciatingly difficult, but I persevered until I achieved a level of expertise that enables me to dance with almost anyone. As soon as I was confident of my ability, I began taking my skills into the "real world" by going to Latin clubs such as the Copacabana, Latin Quarter, and El Flamingo. Naturally, I stand out at these clubs but regard comments such as *bailas bien para un gringo*—"you dance well for a gringo"—as the highest of compliments.

- During the day I may look the part of a successful corporate "suit," but I doubt that my Procter & Gamble officemates would recognize me in my off-hours identity: busker and troubadour. Last week, I played my second gig at Coffee Stages, a coffeehouse-cum-music club on Chicago's North Side. I've performed at open mikes like this one, on and off, for roughly eight years, and in fact have just recorded my first MP3, for release on my Web site, www.MattBrendMusic.com. Still, the highlight of my musical career came when I backpacked through Europe in 2005. At dusk one night on the steps of Madrid's eighteenth-century Monasterio de la Encarnación, I connected with two buskers I heard playing Coldplay tunes on their guitars. Though we couldn't speak each others' languages, we shared musical tastes and a common repertoire. After jamming for hours, they invited me to follow them south to the historic city of Toledo to play in a street musician's festival. For four days, the four of us bounced Radiohead, Coldplay, and Björk tunes off the cobbled walkways and alcoves of this ancient and beautiful town, at times before crowds of 20 to 30 townspeople.

■ Greenpeace is a truly multinational organization: my boss is Dutch, his boss is Irish, and the executive director is German, and every day I work with individuals from Hong Kong, Argentina, Holland, Great Britain, Germany, Nigeria, and Switzerland. Because of my effectiveness working with such diverse teams and my track record for getting results, in 2007 Greenpeace invited me to participate in its worldwide IMPACT initiative to build leadership and change-management skills among Greenpeace's regional directors. I was assigned to work with Greenpeace Malaysia's director and six country managers to develop a new system for building membership and media visibility through Internet and wireless technologies. As part of this change process, I had to assemble and work continuously with a functionally diverse team of people from such areas as law, marketing, technology, and planning. Diversity was not value-added in this project—it was its heart.

■ The cultural open-mindedness that informed my decision to spend a year with the Karanga-Rozvi tribe is the direct result of my international upbringing and my parents' unrelenting efforts to expose my brother, Nir, and me to the cuisine, customs, and lifestyles of other cultures. Growing up as part of the U.S. Navy's extended overseas family at Yokosuka, Japan, and Naples, Italy, I had limitless opportunities to immerse myself in two of the world's richest cultures. While many military-base residents tended to turn inward, succumbing early to "island fever," my parents busily interacted with the local gentry,

➡

exploring local groceries and merchants, learning the language with the gusto of immigrants with no home to return to, and inviting locals into our living room for weekly English lessons. In Yokosuka, this meant that Nir and I gained extensive face time with Japanese children, which eventually triggered our rabid efforts to build the largest collections of manga, anime, and Tamiya auto and robot model kits outside of Greater Nippon.

■ After the 9/11 attack in New York, Anaheim's Muslim community gained attention it did not want or deserve. Overnight, my non-Muslim neighbors became suspicious of the entire Muslim community, though until then we had lived peacefully with each other on the same streets for years. The 9/11 backlash was severe. I can still remember hearing my non-Muslim next-door neighbor tell me that his mother had proclaimed that henceforth no more Muslims would enter her house, though her own daughter had married one! Even in my workplace, I noticed a new wariness and self-imposed segregation divide our Muslim and non-Muslim workforce. Eager to prevent this poisoning of our once collegial workplace, I decided to invite our six Muslim employees to my house for a weekend World Series party. Though some were initially reluctant, all six came, and over the

➡

course of four hours of food and conversation we grew closer. When MediTherapeutics suffered its first war casualty—our sales manager's enlisted son lost his life in Fallujah—our Muslim colleagues were the first to offer Rick their condolences and support.

■ The Israeli army is a melting pot of people from virtually every imaginable background and race. As an officer, the division I led consisted of two Poles, four Moroccans, one Hungarian, two Russians, two Germans, two Iraqis, one Yemeni, and one Egyptian. Such diversity is not unusual. To foster a sense of teamwork in this heterogeneous society, I learned to create opportunities for communication and to nurture each individual's sense of uniqueness. After I had finished my training as a rookie officer, I joined a department where two Russian-born soldiers had fallen behind the others professionally and socially because of their poor Hebrew skills. I got two other soldiers to join me in teaching the language to them, and they quickly got the hang of it and began to integrate into the group. Soon other soldiers were volunteering to take part in our educational operation. Five months later, the two Russian soldiers were promoted to managerial positions. I'll bring this same instinct to reach across cultural barriers to my Stanford Medical School classmates.

➡

■ As a son of a French-trained World Bank expert in animal genetics, I had an international life virtually from birth. I spent my first five years in a diverse, multilingual research community in Azerbaijan where my friends and neighbors ranged from Azerbaijanis and Russians to Brits and Indians. When I was six, we moved to Kuala Lumpur, but I continued to seek out international experiences. At 14, I served as a cultural guide for the Burmese team in the All-South Asian Games, meeting people from all over the continent. When I was 16, I spent a summer in London working for McDonald's, where I gained my first lesson in business and interacted with people from the United States, France, Brazil, and Holland. When I moved to New York City for college, I immediately felt at home in Manhattan's world-embracing diaspora. I want to learn and practice medicine in America because its "melting pot" culture matches the substance and spirit of my "melting pot" life.

■ In high school, my English teacher counseled us all to strive to be "Renaissance men." The ideal of the well-rounded citizen-leader struck a deep chord in me, and in the years since I have tried to live an eclectic life of creativity, public service, leadership, and intellectual accomplishment. At the University of Washington, for example, I joined Amnesty International as a research

➥

officer and learned the importance of careful research and intellectual rigor. My work in traditional Spanish dance and my 10 years of formal music study developed my creative faculties, and as a sometime professional pianist I have performed with the Dallas Youth Symphony, the Seattle Kamerata, and Santa Barbara Mozarteum. Similarly, as an organizer for Pink Jeep Tours of Arizona, I honed my leadership skills organizing outdoor adventures in Sedona, from hot-air balloon trips to horseback trail rides. Closer to my professional life, I have worked as a lab assistant at the University of Washington department of oncology and with the university's department of radiology.

■ In overcoming the traumas of my childhood, I have learned how to lead from health-care industry CEOs like HCA's Jack O. Bovender Jr. and Tenet Healthcare's Trevor Fetter, foreign ambassadors, and church leaders. I have interacted successfully with poor Indonesian city kids, American farmers' sons, and Costa Rican migrant workers. I have caught (carefully) piranha and crocodiles in Venezuela's rivers, defended gay employees from abuse in a Wal-Mart call center, cataloged Russian Orthodox religious icons for a private collector, and taken a three-month sabbatical to travel Sri Lanka with a Tamil student. The core value that will inform my contribution to Washington

➡

University School of Medicine is this: If my own life can encompass so much, then I owe it to my Washington peers to share my message of faith in personal potential; openness to others, diversity, and change; and the joyful pursuit of personal passions.

Chapter 14 Perfect Social Impact Phrases

"What has been the ONE most important volunteer work you have done and why was it meaningful?"

(UCLA)

An all-too-common theme in many medical school admissions essays is the applicants' desire to become a doctor so they can benefit society and help people. It's an admirable goal, but one that medical schools will view skeptically unless there's evidence in the applicants' background that they have acted on that desire. Secondary essays about social impact or volunteer experiences give you the opportunity to do just that. If you have not written about your volunteer clinical experiences in health-care settings elsewhere in your application, social impact essay questions can be a good place to include them. If you have described your clinical experiences, use the social impact topic to show the schools that medical contexts are not the only ones in which you've "given back."

■ My most profound experience of medicine's healing power was completely unplanned. I first met Campbell through a one-on-one social development program in which we met twice a week at the Downtown Athletic Club to run and lift weights. Although, unbeknownst to me, Campbell had been diagnosed with schizophrenia, he seemed no different from anyone else: he sweat from running, burned from lactic acid buildup, and tired from exertion. During the four months we worked together, our relationship grew beyond the confines of the gym. Campbell was an avid painter, and at exhibitions of his work he taught me the finer points of art. I still remember my first lesson. Campbell grabbed my hand, quickly introduced me to his parents, and proceeded to explain the interactions between the colors on every canvas. The thought that he might be a schizophrenic never crossed my mind until our last day together. Casually, in the locker room, Campbell told me that since working with me, he had needed to take less medication. The effect of this statement on me was profound. I had always seen Campbell as a friend I was happy to meet, not as a patient I was "treating." I realized then that the domain of healing is not limited to traditional medical treatments; it can be as simple as being a good friend.

■ When I was finishing my junior year at Baylor, I saw a flyer recruiting instructors to teach swimming and water therapy to developmentally and physically disabled people. My first thought was, "I couldn't possibly do that." But when I realized that my reaction stemmed from fears about and prejudices toward an unfamiliar group of people, I knew I had to apply. I quickly grew to love the place and the people. I still remember the first time Jamal, the center's autistic child with the worst behavior, responded to my therapy by swimming all his laps without splashing others or running out of the pool. Even the routine events—like helping cerebral palsy victims with their daily walks in the pool or chatting with them about their day—made me feel good. My initial fears turned into joy, and my prejudices dissolved into profound respect for these people who coped so bravely with challenges greater than most of us will ever face. In discovering how much I enjoyed working with people who have physical needs, I began to consider a career in medicine.

■ For the past four years, I have worked as an attendant helping handicapped students who need assistance with their daily routines. During the summers I have taught fifth- and sixth-grade science to students who lack adequate educational opportunities. While the

➡

impact of these achievements doesn't qualify me as Mother Theresa, I am proud of the positive differences I have made in others' lives. More than that, I am grateful for the life lessons I have learned from the people whose lives I have touched. From the first day I met Isabelle Kubichek, a disabled Dartmouth student, I could tell I was working with an amazing person, one who had discovered happiness in life despite the tremendous adversity she faced from cerebral palsy. Isabelle's smile and cheery laugh told me that she could easily find the silver lining in any difficult situation. In the four years I have worked with Isabelle, she has taught me to appreciate the simple things in life—that I have a roof to sleep under, food in the refrigerator, and loving friends and family. Without these essentials other things are inconsequential. If I perform poorly on an exam after putting in my best effort, there's no need to worry—there's always another chance to bounce back. I'm lucky. In fact, we're all lucky. "We just need to look at things from the right angle." That's what Isabelle always says.

■ One day in my junior year at Loyola University, Steve Boone, one of my best friends and a Choctaw Native American, made me aware that although the Native American population of Louisiana is 1 percent, there were only two Native Americans at Loyola. We talked with the admissions office and discovered that Loyola organized recruiting trips to Chicago and Los Angeles but didn't visit Louisiana's Native American reservations. A week later we started a campus chapter of the Native American Students Association to raise awareness of the culture of Louisiana's major tribes on campus. More than 50 students and faculty members eventually became actively involved. During Native American Week, we erected an authentic Tunica-Biloxi tribal lodge on campus, brought in Chitimacha dancers from St. Mary Parish, passed out Indian fry bread, and showed historical documentaries daily in the student commons. This not only attracted attention from Loyola's admissions office but from the local community as well. Local grade schools organized field trips to see our lodge and eat the fry bread, and hundreds of New Orleanians came to the Loyola campus to watch the Native American dancers perform.

■ Today, I see my work as an operating room assistant and as a youth counselor at the Samaritan Youth Shelter as two sides of the same coin. As a counselor I am a role model for disadvantaged youths. My responsibility is not only to get the chores done, but to ensure through my words, behavior, and example that the young people learn and grow. "Treatment"

➡

happens every moment of every day. But the shelter's youths are not the only ones growing; I am too. Sexual and drug abuse are difficult topics for young people to confront, but they must. And in helping them address them, I must also understand and honestly confront myself. You cannot tell a client that he has to do something unless you believe inside that he truly does have to do it. You cannot encourage him to share his true feelings if you secretly believe that it is not okay to tell people how you feel. You cannot teach young people to respect themselves if you don't respect yourself first.

■ During my sophomore year in college I began teaching first- to third-grade students every Sunday in my neighborhood church in Salt Lake City, Utah. Though officially my job was to give them bible lessons, I soon discovered that teaching involved more than delivering knowledge. Whether it was young Matthew's puzzled stare or Monica's distracted attention as she watched a fly buzzing on the classroom window, my students quickly informed me that I was simply not reaching them. So I decided to adopt a new approach: to learn as much as I could about each student no matter how busy I was outside class. I was going to connect! In the weeks that followed I made a point of talking to them after class,

➡

playing with them, knowing their favorite snacks and their favorite TV characters. Our communication began to improve tremendously, and Matthew and Monica soon began eagerly participating in class and sharing their feelings. Teaching made my lifelong but until-then inchoate desire to serve people—to help them—concrete. Over time, I decided to combine this new sense of purpose with my enjoyment of the sciences to become a doctor, so I could help people to even greater effect.

■ I felt more than saw Mary Lou Durham's gaze follow me across her hospital room, and I knew the moment of truth was at hand. She was a septuagenarian with both legs recently amputated above the knee, and I was a squeamish 13-year-old volunteer at Tulsa St. Anthony Medical Center's physical therapy department, one of the few patient areas accessible to someone my age. Should I look at her? What if she looked back? Should I even walk by her wheelchair? Perhaps I had made a mistake by asking to be here. I was assigned to assist the therapists, yet here I was failing my first test of compassion. Then—eye contact. To my surprise, Mrs. Durham greeted me with a smile and a simple request, "Tall feller, could you git me a glass of water, please?" I nervously hustled up to her wheelchair with the styrofoam cup, and as she reached out for it, with her free hand she gently held my arm. She understood. Eight years later, though I am 800 miles away from Mrs. Durham, the lesson in compassion of her simple gesture remains with me.

■ Sitting on my desk is a photo of Christopher, an adorable 10-year-old whose huge winning smile boasts his enjoyment of a day at the Albuquerque Zoo. I smile when I see it because I know it tells only half the story. Ten minutes after the photo was taken my little friend burst into tears, started shrieking at the top of his lungs, and vigorously tried to bite me. After college, I accepted a position as a teaching assistant at the Schwinn Developmental School, a private special education school in Albuquerque, where I work in a medically supervised classroom for autistic children with severe developmental delays. Not only are my students nonverbal and low functioning, but they also have intense behavioral problems. Christopher, the student I work with most intimately, throws tantrums during which he bites, hits, scratches, and head-butts the people around him. He arrived in our classroom after a four-month hospitalization. During that time, specialists utilized different drug treatments and behavior modification techniques to attempt to improve his condition. My role is to continue delivering the care outlined by the teacher and members of the medical case–management team with whom I meet weekly. Specifically, I run different work stations, design new activities, collect data on Christopher's behaviors and academic performance, and restrain him when necessary according to a protocol approved by an ethics committee. For nine months, I have been with Christopher from the moment his bus arrives until I strap him in for the ride home. The job continues to test my abilities on a variety of levels, but most importantly, it has challenged my understanding of the physician's role by placing me in a situation where I can never hope to completely remedy Christopher's autism. In working with him, I have to accept even the smallest successes in improving his quality of life as major milestones. Everyone hopes that drug and behavioral therapy will give Christopher greater independence and allow him to experience things we take for granted, such as sitting through a movie or spending a day at the zoo. Nevertheless, the reality is that Christopher's current treatment may at best only delay his move into a full-time residential care facility once his parents can no longer physically handle his violent outbursts. With that in mind, what has my work done for Christopher? As an idealistic college graduate who thought I had all the answers, I was forced to deal with this question, just as Christopher's parents had to deal with it years ago. Although the parents and teachers with whom I work constantly give me reassurance about the quality and value of my efforts, it has taken me a long time to accept the idea that successful healing does not necessarily lead to a cure.

- Volunteering on two mission trips near Torreón, a Mexican city eight hours from the U.S. border, fortified my determination to become a physician. Seeing firsthand the impoverished citizens living by the barest means—barren country farms, just enough running water and food to survive—put my own disappointments into perspective. As we distributed used clothing, basic medicine, and food to the people of La Partida, I noticed how small acts of charity, hand signals, smiles, and laughter overcame the language barrier. Each time we entered a village, the church bells would ring out to signal our arrival. The gratitude these hard-working, religious people showed me was moving and inspiring. I was surprised to find that helping people who really needed it could have as powerful an impact on me as it did on them.

- In 1995 I volunteered for Yount Labs' Blood Borne Pathogen response team, which is responsible for cleaning up bodily fluid spills caused by accidents or injuries. By interacting with patients experiencing health problems, I learned how to remain calm, be reassuring, and efficiently perform physical checks without disturbing the patient. Invigorated by the immediate feedback and gratitude our patients gave me, I began volunteering during my lunch hour to teach disadvantaged children how to play basketball through the Davenport Hoops Foundation. To free up the time for this lunchtime commitment, I would arrive at work early and stay late. On the last day of class, I wished my 12 young students luck and told them I'd see them the next summer. One student, Brayden, came up to me and, while giving me a hug, told me that he didn't think he would see me next summer. His parents weren't sure, he said, that they could afford to send him, and he wanted to say good-bye just in case. I was deeply touched by Brayden's gratitude and emotion. I knew it was the kind of moment I would never experience in my chemistry career but would encounter often as a physician.

- In 2004 I earned my paramedic patch and started teaching advanced cardiac life support (ACLS) and pediatric advanced life support (PALS) classes. The next year, I used my media production skills to build training materials for the Take a Shot for Health immunization program. Soon after, Medi-Redy Rescue asked me to join its team, which gave me even more opportunities to volunteer my time to teaching and participating in EMS. During the Hurricane Katrina devastation, my shock was punctuated by moments of pride as victims were rescued from the engulfed rooftops by fire fighters I had worked with in class just days before. The humbling satisfaction that comes from working with others to save lives is now something I can't live without.

■ I originally got involved in community service activities at Texas Tech to satisfy my parents' expectations. Cofounding Tech's Pet Fanciers Club, I recruited 78 members to sponsor dog and cat shows in the Lubbock area. And twice a month I tutored high school students in the inner city. Enjoying the way volunteer groups spawn friendships and a feeling of accomplishment, in my sophomore year I led six students in organizing events that raised $5,000 for The Safe Place, a nonprofit that provides shelter and support for runaway teens. By my junior year, I was volunteering to be a dorm advisor, even over my parents' protests that it would take too much time away from my studies. Creating a "social impact" theme on my floor of 30 residents, I organized more than six trips to food banks, elementary schools, and nursing homes. By my senior year the community life that had begun out of obedience to my parents had blossomed into an internship for U.S. Congressman Randy Neugebauer, for whom I handle social-work cases involving worker's comp, food stamps, and unemployment training.

■ To convince the dean that a new strategy was essential, I helped coordinate an electronic brainstorming session to which I invited former admissions officers, active alumni, former student admissions assistants, and professors who had reviewed applications for the admissions committee in the past. As the moderator, I got the group to identify the key challenges facing the graduate school's admissions process and to debate needed modifications. After the meeting, I summarized the group's observations, developed a new strategy for improving marketing reach and increasing yield, and vetted the summary with each of the participants. By creating an environment in which admissions challenges could be discussed in a nonthreatening and collaborative way, I was able to convince the dean to approve all six of my recommendations with only minor changes.

■ It was during the second month of my Peace Corps stint in Sironko, Uganda, that Fabayo, our office's maid and cook, mentioned that she was sending her eight-year-old son, Adofo, to work for a blacksmith. I tried to picture little Adofo engulfed in the heat and hazard of a blacksmith's shop and was appalled. Always struggling on their $400 annual income, Fabayo and her husband, a carpenter, had already pulled four of their children out of school so they could learn trades to support themselves. Now Adofo was to be the fifth. Since Fabayo and her husband's parents had done the same to them, they simply had no idea that staying in school might earn their children even better livelihoods as adults. Because the schools in Sironko could not teach the community's children for free and most poor families could not afford the tuition, I decided to organize free elementary education classes for kids like Adofo. First, I created an infrastructure—classrooms, teachers, books—by making strategic donations to locals in exchange for use of a makeshift classroom and the part-time teaching assistance of a nearby missionary organization. Three weeks after conceiving my plan, the Sironko school started class with seven children.

- I'm particularly proud of the policy change I implemented last year in the Dover Free Clinic's treatment of strep throat. This disease can cause a sore throat in children, but more importantly it can also cause heart damage. Treating it effectively and quickly is critical. While the previous clinic policy, drug treatment, was effective, the drug's high cost meant we could rarely get enough donations from pharmaceutical companies to serve our population. I researched the medical literature and consulted with infectious disease specialists and local epidemiologists as well as the state public health department. Armed with my findings, I convinced the clinic to change the protocol from the expensive drug to a much cheaper but equally efficacious one that was available in generic form and that pharmaceutical companies were much happier to donate in larger quantities.

Chapter 15 Perfect Phrases
for Conclusions

An effective conclusion can do several things at once. It can offer a wise, amusing, or self-knowing lesson from your essay's stories in an unhackneyed, forward-looking way that seems organic to and yet an enhancement of what's come before. It can give your essay a sense of formal closure, and it can show how the experiences you've focused on in your essay connect to your decision to go to medical school. Here are some perfect phrases for essay conclusions.

- As the health-care delivery system moves away from decisions made solely between individual physicians and their patients, more and more medical industry resources will be focused on the bottom line, a balance sheet that has no line marked compassion. In that quantified future, who will speak for the Mrs. Jorgensons, the Juan Pazes, the Katie Bondses? I will.

- Perhaps this idea was summed up most succinctly by a doctor who worked in an emergency room where

I used to volunteer: "Sometimes a day goes by so fast that the cases seem to blur together in my mind, but to the patients each interaction with their doctor is hugely magnified," he said. "You become a major presence in their lives." Rising to the responsibility of that magnified role is why I want to become a doctor.

■ John Donne wrote, "Death be not proud. For those whom thou think'st thou dost overthrow, Die not, poor Death." Even though Alex is gone, he lives on in my aspiration to help others. In four months I will obtain my full Red Cross certification, and my volunteer work at St. Louis Memorial is already strengthening my understanding of patients' clinical needs. This fall I will continue my research into grade IV brain tumors in Dr. Ordway's lab. Alex's friendship taught me the deathless lesson that we can make a difference by cultivating the skills and mindset to enhance human life. As a physician, I can enact Donne's words every day of my career.

■ I believe an officer on a navy submarine is not unlike a surgeon in the operating room. Concentrating while under stress, coordinating complex procedures, deploying sophisticated technologies, projecting cool leadership, and understanding human relationships inform the surgeon's success just as they have mine as a sub commander. Having excelled in one ultimate and intensely real form of leadership has been superb preparation for the challenges of the other.

- "Some of the greatest things in life come from doing what others say you cannot." I read these words in a fortune cookie once, and I have lived by them ever since. Just as I proved in my swimming career that I can face down adversity and accomplish great things by following my heart, I am eager now to see where the strength of my focus and dedication will take me as a physician. Medicine is the best way for me to serve and express the compassion I have been raised with while also challenging me, just as swimming has. I am excited about the challenges I will face in medical school.

- Two years later, I found myself back in a doctor's office, this time with literally my whole life hanging on the words of a multiple sclerosis specialist. She put her arm around me and paused before smiling and saying, "Candace, it's always nice to give people good news." And with that, the power of a second opinion, the uncertainty of nine months vanished, and my final test, like a mountain being lifted from my shoulders, was over. I believe each test has led me closer and more confidently toward a career in medicine. Nothing can stop me now.

- Through my varied professional experiences, I have come to realize that the practice of medicine is as much an art as a science; that compassion and caring are often more important to the patient than the latest treatment option or technology; that personality, communication, and social skills are as central to a good physician's role as medical knowledge. My long and winding professional road has brought me to the gates of medicine. I am uniquely prepared to enter and to succeed.

- My physician father's example has taught me a lot. But it's been on my own that I've learned that medicine is only partly about illness. It's also one of the best ways to make people happy.

- Six years ago in Barisal, Bangladesh, I encountered disease caused by famine, overcrowding, poor sanitation, pollution, and inattention, and I was neither able to understand it nor treat it. To truly understand these scourges, I have studied both biological and environmental sciences at Oxford and in jungles on three continents. But to truly treat these diseases, I must go to medical school.

- I have learned that culture, ethnicity, social environment, feelings, and beliefs all influence a person's health and response to treatment. In a country as diverse as the United States, eliminating the disparities in health care will mean understanding all these factors—being sensitive to differences so we can, yes, value them but primarily so we can respond effectively to them. Achieving that understanding will be the goal of my medical education and of my career.

- In the end, I learned not to regret my decision to repeat my experience in Irrawaddy Delta, Myanmar, and instead embraced, once again, the new, untried challenge. I know my next, biggest challenge will be medical school and—once again—I will be ready.

- This drive to fully realize all my passions has brought me today to the decision to dedicate myself to medicine. I want a career that will not force me to choose between my love of people and my passion for science. Every job or activity I have truly enjoyed has been people-intensive, and both my research internships and my pharmacology major have sharpened my vested interest in the science of body and mind. Everything that drives me comes together in medicine.

- My study of neuroscience has given me an acute knowledge of the physiological effects of controlled substances on the brain, and I know from all-too-personal experience the toll that drug addiction takes on families. My brother still battles to stay sober, and I see his face in the struggles of all the addicts I have worked with. I made a promise to return to the clinic as a doctor some day. As I prepare to intern at

➥

the Betty Ford Center this May, I know it is a promise
I will keep.

- All I could do that day in the ER was wipe the blood
from the boy's head and nose. With a medical degree
I will be able to do so much more. Doctors hold the
gift of life in their hands. I seek the training to be able
to give that gift to everyone who seeks it from me.

- I believe becoming a truly healing physician means
achieving an intimate marriage of compassion,
knowledge, and the capacity to see the world in an
open, more expansive way. It is these qualities that
underlie my experiences in such broadly different
settings as the New Jordan Counseling Center,
destitute rural Costa Rica, an inner-city ER in
New Jersey, and the world of research into
neurodegenerative disorders. As a physician I can
continue to traverse and understand different worlds
and, better yet, make my own contribution to them.

- I have been surrounded by physicians in my work and
academic life since the end of college. They have
deeply impressed me with the sheer variety of skills
they must bring to their professional role. But more
than that, they have impressed me with the
responsibility they have earned to affect—and
sometimes save—the lives of people like Justin and
Angelina. My experiences in bench research, clinical

trials, patient interaction, and drug development have given me the absolute confidence that I can also earn that responsibility to heal.

■ Dr. Goodwin's unexpected death last year means that, unfortunately, I will no longer be able to share with him my ambitions for the calling he selflessly served for five decades. But his impact on my future career has already been enormous. My childhood memories of his hearty laugh and trademark pipe will always remind me of the "old-fashioned" medicine I also hope to practice: healing through the power of knowledge and a gentle, humane touch.

■ Scientific advances are the foundation upon which actual patient treatment practices evolve. Today, I know I don't have to make a choice between my passion for research and serving others—they are the same thing.

■ I have deliberately tested my commitment to medicine and have always come back to the same essential fact: medicine will help me use my natural strengths to improve the lives of others while I do something that I love. I look forward to the challenges and discoveries ahead with optimism and purpose.

■ When I entered the family waiting lounge, Frederique's mother hugged me so hard she nearly knocked me over. In that one embrace, my long years of studying, clinical volunteer work, and EMT experiences suddenly fell into perspective. At 11 p.m. on a Saturday night, when most people are enjoying their weekend, studying biochemical pathways and arcane tidbits of pathology can seem an odd use of one's time. Frederique's mother crystallized for me why I want to use mine in medical school: I want to help protect others' health. Her hug told me I would.

Part IV

Perfect Phrases for Interviews

Chapter 16 Perfect Phrases for Medical School Interviews

The interview invitation is one of the decisive winnowing moments in the medical admissions process. While some schools will send everyone who applies a secondary application, usually only the applicants who have a serious chance at admission will receive an interview invite. When the journal *Academic Medicine* asked medical schools which of five factors (including MCAT scores, science and nonscience grade-point average, and recommendation letters) mattered most in their decision to admit an applicant, they ranked the interview as the most important. Medical schools use the interview to see if you have the social and communication skills and balanced personality to succeed in medical school and as a physician. It also enables them to see if you match the person you've presented in your essays and application. If there is anything unusual or troublesome in your profile, you can bet you will be asked about it in the interview. The range of questions the interviewers may ask you is huge, so in the following perfect phrases we've included only those types of questions that applicants most often encounter.

Tell me about yourself.

■ "Sure. Though I was born and raised in a middle-class
family in Peoria, Illinois, I've led a pretty unusual life.
When I was 10, my father took a sabbatical from his
teaching job and bought a sailboat, which he and my
mother, sister, and I sailed around the Caribbean for
two years. The exposure I gained to the cultural variety
of that region was an incredible eye-opener for me,
and ever since then I have been a travel nut. So far I've
traveled to 16 countries, and I've lived or worked in
Norway, Panama, and the United Kingdom. I speak
three languages fluently: English, Norwegian, and
German. When I was 16, my family moved to Oslo,
Norway, which was a bit difficult for me at first
because of the cold winters and language barrier.
I worked hard at learning Norwegian and eventually
made friends who showed me Scandinavia's "hot"
spots and backpacked with me through Europe,
including Russia. When I was 18, I began having
trouble concentrating in class and keeping up my
energy. I went to a doctor when I began having
frequent headaches, nausea, and numbness, and he
ordered comprehensive MRI scans, which indicated
possible multiple sclerosis. During the six months
I spent waiting for more conclusive tests and a
differential diagnosis, I learned everything I could

about MS and its treatment. By the time I got the good news—my symptoms were actually Lyme disease—I had already decided to go to med school and become a neurosurgeon. I knew I wanted to exploit the advances in high-precision computer navigational technology that are making possible brain surgery for controlling the movement disorders common in multiple sclerosis. That's basically why I'm sitting here today."

What do you do for fun?

■ "I play and listen to Carnatic music, an ancient form of Indian classical music. It consists mainly of devotional songs composed centuries ago to praise Hindu gods or to pray for health, peace, and wealth. It can be played on accompanying instruments such as the violin and a percussion instrument called the miruthangam, but it can also be very expressive and moving on its own. I first learned it from my mother when I was a child, and by my teens I was performing it at neighborhood concerts. I started a Carnatic music club at Grinnell College and still give lessons to anyone who wants to learn. I find that Carnatic music really encourages soul-searching and helps me

➡

achieve a rational calm and synchronize my body and mind. I know it's going to help me deal with the pressures of medical school!"

- "When I was 18, two friends and I jumped on a Greyhound bus and spent eight weeks traveling through California, Nevada, Utah, and Wyoming. Discovering Native American art at the reservations we passed through, I really connected with the emphasis that Hopis, Navahos, and Zunis place on worshipping nature and community. The beautiful ceramics and statuary that reflect Native Americans' sacred vision charmed and fascinated me. Today, my apartment is chock-full of Native American blankets, pottery, and figures, and last fall I launched NativeArtWays.org, a blog and trading platform for Native art connoisseurs."

Cholesterol is a precursor of which hormone?

- "Estrogen, a steroid hormone."

Where in the nephron is most reabsorption of glucose likely to occur?

- "Sorry, I don't know the answer to that. But I'd be glad to tell you about my tissue engineering. Today, my research team at the University of Tennessee is improving vascular grafts by seeding the luminal layer of an expanded polytetrafluroethylene tube with endothelial cells. Because these cells have antithrombogenic factors and prevent intimal hyperplasia, vascular surgeons can use these synthetic grafts below the current 6-millimeter internal diameter limit. Using a unique electrostatic seeding device we developed, our team is testing the effectiveness of the seeding under in vitro and in vivo conditions. Spending hours working with surgeons as they implant our grafts has been exciting for me, and I look forward to continuing my research into genetically engineered endothelial cells in the years ahead."

What are you proudest of?

■ "Probably, that I excelled in a nationally ranked Division I collegiate swimming program. Three years ago I made it my goal to lift my swimming to its highest level. I practiced more, swam on school and public teams, and worked with a former Olympic swimming coach. My team at the University of Kentucky has won two conference championships and five conference relay titles, and I've received a most-improved honor and been named to the

Southeastern Conference Scholar Athlete Team and Academic All-Conference Swimming team. Just as important, I've done all this while maintaining a cumulative 3.65 GPA. Just before my senior year Coach Burris told me I had earned a full athletic scholarship—an unusual honor for a nonrecruited athlete. Swimming has shown me that I have the leadership abilities to affect others and the perseverance to succeed at challenges that demand hard work and long-term commitment."

■ "In three-plus years, I've gone from social chair to national liaison for the Washington, DC, chapter of Young Native American Professionals. This past September, I was elected community relations director of YNAP's parent organization, Young Native Americans United, a 24-chapter organization whose current membership exceeds 40,000. As the community relations director, my role is to help young Native Americans get an education and competitive jobs and to increase public perception of young Native Americans as a productive force in all aspects of American life. As a member of the eight-person executive board of YNAU, I am helping the organization expand nationally, spreading the word about our 501(c)3 charitable foundation, and soliciting corporate sponsorship for our scholarship fund for

➡

college-age Native Americans. I'm very pleased with our results and intend to start a YNAP chapter in Madison when you admit me."

Tell me about your research.

■ "I've always enjoyed the sciences and all of my high school lab classes, so I knew my career would somehow involve research. But I wasn't sure which research avenue I should pursue until my childhood friend Shana was diagnosed with tuberculosis the day after my high school graduation. Fortunately, she was not infected with a multidrug-resistant strain and completed her course of prophylactic therapy successfully. I discovered that three million people a year are not so lucky, however, and lose their lives to TB. So I've been fortunate to work with Dr. Linda Zimmerman's lab studying the molecular genetics of mycobacterium tuberculosis. Working my way up to lab student manager, I've had my hand in almost every aspect of our development of a new strain that Dr. Zimmerman is now testing for vaccinogenic potential, from literature searches and writing research protocols to applying for grants, performing experiments, and presenting results at meetings.

➡

Because I have attained first-author status in my first year of graduate school, successfully had a grant application funded, applied for a patent, and presented my work at four conferences and symposiums, Dr. Zimmerman has encouraged me to devote myself to research. But for reasons I'd be glad to discuss, I am committed to becoming a practicing physician."

- "With Dr. Liu Pang, director of the Immunology Research Center, and Dr. Toshiro Toyoshima of UCLA's department of immunology, I have been investigating the connection between sleep and the human immune system. By simultaneously recording the sleep and sampling the lymph and blood of unrestrained sheep, we have demonstrated that during sleep the activity and number of natural killer cells, which play key roles in recognizing tumor and virally infected cells, declines precipitously in the peripheral circulation. This suggested that natural killer cells protectively migrate into the tissues during sleep, indicating that the alteration of normal sleep-wake states could hinder natural killer cell activity and thus result in immune suppression. In 2005, I convinced Dr. Bruce Knauff, a neurophysiologist whose lab was next door to ours, to help me investigate the central nervous system actions of Interleukin–1, a substance with both immune-supporting and sleep-inducing properties. Over two summers, I discovered that the prevailing notion that Interleukin–1 mediated sleep and fever only in pathological circumstances was false—it could also affect neurotransmission at levels found in the normal brain. Because brain Interleukin–1 levels are highest just before sleep Interleukin–1 could play a role in regulating normal sleep processes. Our results have also indicated that subtle changes in brain IL–1 levels can significantly hinder the nervous system's ability to relay messages. This may be one of the causes of AIDS-related dementia and chronic fatigue syndrome, where patients have increased levels of IL–1. The potential ramifications of our research are very exciting."

Why did you choose the undergraduate institution you did?

■ "My high school was the typical American suburban high school where jocks and conformity rule and intellectual, creative, or unusual people—like me—were considered 'nerds' and social outcasts. Without really being conscious of it, I think I looked for a university where I would feel at home with other people like me. I made visits to a couple of Big Ten campuses, but didn't

➡

really feel they were different from my high school environment. I still remember the day I toured the University of Chicago's campus in Hyde Park with my dad. The guy who showed us around was an articulate, bespectacled type, sort of nerdy but with attitude —my type. And the campus itself is full of Oxbridge-style architecture, so it appealed to my desire for something a little different. As an early decision applicant I applied to no other schools and never regretted that decision. It's true that I struggled a little academically at first, but that was just because I needed to adjust to the rigor of the education Chicago gives you. I eventually graduated with honors. More importantly, in my four years at Chicago I met wonderfully interesting and intelligent people from every part of the world, challenged myself intellectually like I never had before, came out my shell as a leader, and discovered my interest in biomedical informatics."

What specialty appeals to you most? Why? [or] How do you see your future career unwinding?

- "I want a career in emergency medicine because no matter how much you plan, EM is so unpredictable. It's a hands-on specialty that requires fast action and the ability to think on your feet. It offers me a chance to help people in immediate need and maybe even save a life. I also enjoy the diversity of patients and medical conditions and the opportunity to establish rapport with patients and team members under stressful situations. I have also found that I seem to enjoy both the nurses and physicians and the research literature of emergency medicine more than I do other specialties. There's also an openness in emergency medicine, a direct desire to solve problems. The EM physicians I've met are, like me, active people who are fun to be around. And of course, like all medicine, emergency medicine offers me constant, lifelong learning. In six years I imagine I will be an EM physician in a rural setting. I would like to give back to the community not just by working in the emergency department but by giving local talks on exercise, healthy nutrition, and mental training. I'd also like to continue volunteering overseas (perhaps returning to Mexico's Sierra Madre Mountains yearly) so I can enjoy the challenges and rewards of international medicine."

■ "During my mission trips to Nigeria, I was shocked to learn that 90 percent of our cases were children with easily curable ailments like malnutrition, lice, and fungal cases. That's when I began to focus on pediatrics. Helping to lead our church's vacation bible school affirmed my ability to build rapport with little kids. Because of these experiences, I believed that the best way for me to serve was to be a primary care pediatrician with a free clinic in a poor part of the U.S. During my day with Dr. Fawell, however, I asked him what doctors his organization needed most. He replied that while it's true that Africa could use ob/gyns and dermatologists, what he really needed were general surgeons because their internal medicine and surgery skills make them so versatile. Dr. Prescott added that his friend with the *Ship of Health* serving Southeast Asia most requested orthopedic surgeons because of the region's high incidence of polio, leprosy, and other deformity-causing diseases. So I've since opened my career options to include surgery. I want to run a low-fee surgical clinic modeled after the Mercy Center that is integrated with a church so patients can request spiritual help if they wish it. If I choose general surgery, I will run a general surgery clinic while volunteering for Médecins Sans Frontières. If I choose orthopedic surgery, I will run an orthopedic surgical clinic and travel with the *Ship of Health* or other floating hospitals."

■ "Because of my eye-opening experience in a Harlem ER while completing my EMT requirement, I want to spend the first part of my career in a city hospital. Aside from the challenging and diverse patient population, I'll also have the opportunity to continue the neurological research I did at Brandeis. Ten years from now, I may be doing part-time clinical research to help develop pharmaceuticals and pharmaceutical delivery systems or lab research in neuroscience. Outside of my practice I will also continue my volunteer relationship with the American Red Cross, since as a physician I will be able to serve that organization in a much more significant capacity. I plan to maintain my Red Cross certification in disaster services, and I'm also interested in sitting on the board of directors of a local chapter so I can offer a physician's insights. Finally, I want to devote the latter part of my career to serving a rural community like the one I grew up in in Wyoming. I'm very familiar with the special demands and rewards of a rural career. It's a natural place for me to close out my career."

Why do you want to go to our medical school?

- "Mount Sinai has always been on my short list because of its amazing tradition and reputation: consistently high rankings in multiple specialties in

U.S. News and a long history of medical 'firsts'—including the first institution to link cigarettes to cancer and combine radiation and chemotherapy to treat ovarian and breast cancer. But after talking to Mount Sinai alumni and students—including recent grads Morty Gavrilap and Nick Leeson—I began to focus more on Mount Sinai's progressive curriculum. Courses like Art and Science of Medicine and Bench to Bedside will enable me to balance the foundation I gain in the molecular bases of health and disease with exciting clinical experiences. Moreover, Mount Sinai's Personalized Medicine Research Program will enable me to pursue the research interests I have developed at PharmaGen outside of a formal Ph.D. program. Finally, given that two-thirds of Mount Sinai's entering class majored in subjects other than biology, I'm certain that my own nontraditional profile—an education in art history, professional experience in high school teaching, and extensive science bench work—will enable me to thrive."

Why will you be a good doctor?

- "Interesting question. Some people have told me that at 28 years old I'm 'too old' to begin a medical career.

I tell them that I have needed every one of those years to become the person I am—someone who understands the sacrifices you have to make to pursue a dream and understands that medicine is not just a 'career choice' but a chance to use science and technology to deliver hope and care to people. It's true that I've taken the long road to a medical career, but my experiences in university research and nonprofit administration have given me the sympathy, integrity, and dedication I need to be an effective physician."

- "I know that my creativity will help me be a good doctor. At Austin Doctors Hospital, many patients who were initially shy opened up when I shared my art therapy techniques with them. By helping patients to draw or by drawing alongside them, I found that it became much easier to initiate conversations and forge friendships. I think that precisely because each patient is unique, creativity is the crucial ingredient in enabling physicians to make the leap from applying the knowledge learned through lectures and experience to tailoring treatment to fulfill each patient's individual needs. In medical school and afterward I will look for ways to incorporate creativity into the care I provide my patients."

- "Well, on one level I possess both the necessary intellectual skills and exposure to health care to know that I can handle the challenges of a medical career. My undergraduate GPA, my participation in research at the Centers for Disease Control, and my service as secretary and president-elect of Columbia's premedical society speak to my intellectual and experiential preparation. However, it's my ability to connect with others, for example, through humor, that gives me the ultimate confidence that I can become an effective, compassionate, patient-centered physician. Growing up in a small Missouri town whose name was synonymous regionwide for the state's home for the mentally ill, I had to quickly develop the sense of humor to deflect the jokes that always came when I mentioned my hometown! I think all these traits will come together to make me an effective and caring physician."

What do you think is the biggest problem with the U.S. health-care system? How would you fix it?

■ "I was hoping you would ask that because I can't really imagine any more serious health-care problem than the number of uninsured—about 47 million Americans, including my younger brother. I believe health care should be available to anyone who seeks it, but the real question is what is the most effective way to bring it about. I agree with opponents of government-sponsored health care that universal coverage would require higher taxes, would tend to lead to higher costs, and might negatively affect the quality of care provided. But the sheer size of the U.S. population, the impracticality of placing the entire health-care burden on employers or individuals alone, and the example of other countries tells me that government involvement and hence some inefficiency are unavoidable. I think that the answer is some kind of public-private solution that combines coverage for everyone who wants it with built-in incentives and safeguards for cost efficiency and innovation. One solution that seems promising to me is a health insurance system that uses 'risk equalization' methods as in the Netherlands. Health insurance is compulsory there, provided through policies that private insurance companies compete with each other to offer each citizen. Because there's free-market competition, these insurance policies remain affordable. At the same time, no insurance company can deny coverage to someone on the basis of poor health. The government compensates the insurance companies for covering such high-risk citizens. I think this approach might work in the United States because the Dutch government's role is only to incentivize insurance companies to cover everyone. It doesn't push the private sector out of the picture, so free-market efficiencies restrain costs."

Do you have any questions for me?

- "How many students typically pursue second degrees, such as a master's in public health? Is their time off for those degrees integrated into the curriculum and funded by their tuition or do they have to pay extra tuition?"
- "Are any changes to the curriculum planned? Are students given any role in determining these changes?"
- "Am I allowed to send the admissions committee information or materials to update it on my candidacy?"
- "What percentage of students receive their first choice in the residency match, and does the school make the match statistics available?"

Closing Thoughts

Although a 3.85 grade-point average and an MCAT score of 40 will hide a multitude of sins, what you write and say about yourself in your AMCAS and secondary essays will usually be key factors in your chances of being accepted to medical school. The words that succeed with admissions committees are usually the ones that show the most honesty, self-knowledge, creativity, and hard work. Remember this as you consult this and other admissions guidebooks. Admissions officers read books like these too, and they have an uncanny ability (honed on the job) to recall passages they've encountered before. More importantly, they have an uncanny ability to detect when an applicant's essay rings false. For these reasons alone, do yourself a favor and use this book's "ready-to-use" phrases only as models to study, inspirations to emulate, or even first-draft crutches on your way to your own voice. Because in the end, the only perfect phrase is your own.

About the Author

Paul Bodine is the author of *Great Application Essays for Business School, Great Personal Statements for Law School, Perfect Phrases for Business School Acceptance,* and *Perfect Phrases for Law School Acceptance.* One of America's most experienced admissions consultants (serving clients since 1997), he is a graduate of the University of Chicago and Johns Hopkins University and lives in Southern California.